The little big things

The little big things

A young man's belief that

every day can be a good day

HENRY FRASER

SEVEN DIALS

First published in Great Britain in 2017
by Seven Dials
an imprint of The Orion Publishing Group Ltd
Carmelite House, 50 Victoria Embankment
London EC4Y 0DZ

An Hachette UK Company

11

A CIP catalogue record for this book
is available from the British Library.

ISBN: 978 1 4091 6778 5

Printed in Great Britain by CPI Group (UK) Ltd,
Croydon, CR0 4YY

www.orionbooks.co.uk

For my Mum and Dad and brothers, Tom, Will and Dom, who have always been there for me. You have given me so much of your lives so I can live mine. Without you I do not know where I would be right now.

✳

For my friends who have been there for me from the start. You have never seen my disability as a barrier but as a way of creating new memories.

CONTENTS

FOREWORD

HENRY FRASER IS one of the most remarkable people I've ever met.

Prior to the accident that transformed his life, Henry was intelligent, gifted and handsome, which most of us would agree is quite enough to be going on with. Circumstances had not yet arranged themselves to reveal what an exceptional person Henry truly was. Then he went on holiday with his friends, dived into the ocean and everything changed in a second.

I first came across Henry's story by chance. I'd only visited the Saracens rugby club website to check the details of a fixture mentioned in a whodunit I was writing. Henry's story caught my eye and, in the grand tradition of all novelists doing research, I promptly abandoned what I was supposed to be doing to read something far more interesting.

A few weeks later, my friend and agent, Neil Blair, began telling me the story of a young man whom he had just taken on as a client. The story sounded very familiar. 'Neil, this isn't Henry Fraser, is it?'

And so, with a shared agent as my excuse, I got in touch with Henry. We chatted online for a while and finally met at his first art exhibition, which documented his mouth-painting journey from first drawings to beautiful, fully realised paintings. He made a speech that night that will, I'm sure, have stayed with everyone who heard it. His honesty, his modesty, the unflinching way he described both his accident and the way he had adapted to and was making the most of a life he had not expected, were astonishing.

I follow Henry on Twitter and regularly chat with him by Direct Message. Most people respond to him the way I did: admiration tinged with awe. Occasionally, though, I watch him dealing with another kind of attention. One woman told him he was being punished for stupidity in diving into the ocean from the beach. A man jeered at him for conning everyone; how could he use Twitter if he were really paralysed?

You can almost smell the fear in these unsolicited comments. Accepting the reality of Henry's story means thinking about challenges and privations that some find too terrifying to contemplate. Apportioning blame is a way of trying to deflect the simple truth that anybody's existence may undergo a sudden, irreversible, unavoidable change.

We humans are more fragile than we like to think. Fate forced Henry Fraser down a terrifying path for which no preparation was possible. He had to find his own way back to a life worth living and in doing so he revealed himself to be a person of extraordinary perseverance, strength and wisdom. He pushes himself both physically and mentally, exceeding expectations in every direction, raising money for causes he cares about, his art becoming more accomplished with every drawing and painting he produces.

Above all, Henry is living proof that acceptance and aspiration are not mutually exclusive. How many of us can truly say that we accept the present facts of our life, while living it to its fullest extent? It is understandable to rage against present limitations, but sometimes we make them our excuse not to act, not to do all that we can: for ourselves, for others, for the world.

Henry remains intelligent, gifted and handsome, but he is now something more, something rarer: someone truly inspirational. He is remarkable, not for what happened to him, but for what he makes happen. This book is merely his latest achievement, and nobody who knows him doubts that there is much more to come. I'm truly proud to count him one of my friends.

J. K. ROWLING

1

One
Brief
Moment

LIFE WAS GOOD. The first year of sixth form at my new school had been brilliant – the rugby, the social life, the endless sense of adventure and possibility that came with being in London – and when my new mates asked me to go on holiday after our summer exams, I didn't hesitate in accepting. We were a close group hanging around together in and out of school, on and off the rugby pitch, and a week in the sun in a villa in Praia da Luz seemed like a great way of ending the school year.

I nearly hadn't made it. At the boarding gate – having got through baggage *and* security – the attendant checking the boarding passes told me I couldn't get on the plane as my passport had expired. My bag was unloaded and I had to turn around, walk the walk of shame, go right back past the boarding gates and take a return train to Hertfordshire, thinking there was no way I was now going to make it to Portugal. Fortunately, my parents were understanding. We'd not travelled abroad much as a family and so it hadn't occurred to any of us to check my passport before I left. When I arrived back home, fed up and disappointed, I told my mum that I might as well not go as it was going to be such a hassle to get me out there in time. But they could see how much this holiday meant to me and they did what kind parents do. My dad took the day off work so he and I could go to Liverpool, the nearest place – over 200 miles from my house – where we could get a fast-tracked new passport, while my mum arranged for a new ticket to Portugal, and without much fuss at all I joined my friends in time for dinner the next night.

And I was made up to be there. Naturally shy and

often happier in my own company, I had adapted well to my new school. Following in my brother Will's footsteps, I had been accepted, after my GCSEs, as a weekly boarder at Dulwich College on a sports scholarship and had played for a year in the First XV as a flanker-cum-centre. Most of my friends came from the squad and it meant a great deal to me to have been accepted as part of the team, both on and off the field.

Arriving in Portugal a day late didn't really make much difference – though I was stuck with a mattress that might as well have been packed with concrete – and I soon slotted in and picked up on the rhythm of the holiday: sleeping in till late, having breakfast, going down to the beach to chuck a rugby ball about, sunbathing, swimming and chilling, and then going back to the villa to cook together. My friends Marcus and Hugo had been coming to this particular spot on the Algarve for years and had got friendly with locals and regulars around the same age. In the evenings we would meet up with some of their friends for a night out in Lagos, rolling home in the early hours, once or twice in time for sunrise. This was my first adult-free holiday abroad and I was determined to live every second, day and night.

On the fifth day, like all the other days before, we were down at the beach playing a bit of football-rugby. It was mid-afternoon and the beach was alive with families; children playing, running in and out of the sea. The sun was fierce and hot and when it became too much, Rory and Marcus ran into the sea to cool down. I'd already been swimming earlier and knew how refreshing that water was. Seeing them go, I suddenly craved that moment when, head under, my body would recover from the heat. I chased after them, dodging the children making sandcastles on the flat, wet part of the beach.

I ran into the sea until it was waist-high and then, as I had already done hundreds of times that week, dived in. But, this time, as I came down, I crashed my head on the seabed. Opening my eyes, I found myself floating below the surface of the water, face down, my arms hanging lifeless in front of me, unable to move anything from below my neck. The silence of the sea piercing my ears was the most terrifying sound I have ever heard. I couldn't move and I couldn't breathe and even though it was only a matter of seconds, it felt like forever. I was scared and helpless. Swearing over and over, desperate for a way to stay alive and catch a breathe. I thought that was it for me.

I heard Marcus asking me if I was OK. I heard Hugo shout: 'Frase, stop messing about. Catch this,' as a ball hit the water. I needed to tell them I wasn't messing about and just managed to turn my head slightly to one side – a minute movement that both saved my life and irreparably changed it – and get my mouth half out of the water to say, 'Help me.' I heard Hugo shout to Marcus and together they dragged me through the sea onto the beach and laid me down on my back. By this time all my mates were standing above me, their expressions unable to hide their panic. 'Sorry, guys,' I managed, 'I think I may have ruined the holiday.' Before they could say anything, I felt someone take hold of my head, telling me not to move a thing. Two English guys – ex-rugby coaches as it happens – had seen me being dragged out of the water and had come over to help. They lifted and slid me very carefully onto a bodyboard, and covered me with towels to stop me shaking from cold. Stuart, who introduced himself while holding my head, told me, calmly and firmly, not to panic, that it was probably just a compressed neck and that an ambulance was on its way. He asked me if I could move my right hand and I found that I could. Later, I was told this was my body in spasm, the movement totally involuntary.

The strange thing was that at first I really wasn't panicking and it was as if everything was happening in slow motion. I could still hear the sea, could still hear kids splashing and laughing, could still feel the sun on my face. But as the minutes ticked by and I still couldn't feel *a thing*, couldn't move a muscle, I was overcome with terror. I had a parallel vision of myself getting up and carrying on as before while at the same time being rigid with the realisation that something very, very bad was happening.

Then things moved quickly. The paramedics arrived, put my neck in a brace, lifted me onto a stretcher and took me to another part of the beach where a helicopter was waiting to airlift me to hospital. My friends ran alongside me and I asked if Marcus could come with me, but he was held back by the paramedics. By this time I was panicking out loud, not yet numb from the trauma, and if it hadn't been for the paramedic who held my hand and talked to me all the time – her broken English soft and kind – the journey would have been a whole lot worse. She told me that I was doing great, breathing for myself, and that I was going to the best hospital in Lisbon where I would be seen by the best doctors and that, whatever was happening, it would all be OK. As I was learning, the kindness of strangers is a wonderful thing.

Just as you see on TV hospital dramas, my trolley was crashed through the A&E doors where the medical staff were waiting for me. My paramedic said goodbye and wished me luck and, as she left, I felt an overwhelming sense that nobody knew where I was. I wanted my parents more than anything. There was a lot of talk going on above and around me that I wasn't able to understand and I asked if I could use the phone to call my parents. But there was no time. They needed to get me straight into X-ray. This took a matter of moments and I think I might have zoned out a bit because the next thing I felt was cream being smeared on the sides of my face and then what felt like – and, it turned out, actually were – screws being inserted on either side of my head. I was hooked into a big metal brace, a sort of halo over my head, and clamped onto a pulley system that had weights attached to it. In stretching my neck, the doctors hoped that my fourth vertebra – which was now completely out of alignment – would slide back into place. Time would tell.

I longed for my parents. I didn't know if anyone in the world knew where I was. That morning I had been frying eggs for breakfast, the only mild worry in my mind how I'd done in my AS Levels, and now here I was, immobile, covered in sand, in a totally strange bed with twenty kilos hanging off my neck. As I watched the clock count down the seconds, I drifted out of one nightmare into another and then another as the nurse assigned to me held my hand.

※

THOUGH I DIDN'T KNOW IT, during that first fitful night my parents were on their way to me. Assuming I'd been taken off the beach to the local hospital in Portimão, as one of the medics had told them, my friends had spent the rest of the day frantically searching for me and it was only much later when, by chance, they bumped into one of the paramedics who had been on the beach, that she put two and two together and told them that I was three hundred kilometres away in Lisbon. There are four hospitals in Lisbon, so with the help of Marcus and Hugo's Portuguese-speaking friends, they finally managed to track me down at São José. They had then called Marcus's dad, who is a doctor, and he had broken the news to my parents.

Arriving at the hospital my parents asked to see me straight away, but were told I wasn't 'ready' and were instead taken to see the surgeon who, without hesitation, told them that I had severed my spinal cord and that I would never again be able to walk or use my arms; that I was going to be a tetraplegic for the rest of my life. To this day, I cannot imagine the shock my parents experienced. They had last seen me happily dashing out of the front door, waving my new passport, excited to be leaving. I am the third of four brothers and our lives were dominated by sport and activity. Someone was always on the move, going off to or coming back from a run or a swim or rugby practice, the four of us, as well as my mum and dad, full of energy and motion. Activity was our thing.

My mum told me later – much later – that while my dad's reaction had been one of such alarm he'd been unable even to speak, she'd started screaming. And that after she had screamed for a few seconds, the surgeon had the presence of mind – and years of grim experience – to tell both my parents that this was the time when I would need them more than ever. That from the minute I saw them, they would need to summon every bit of strength they had ever had and be as resilient and positive as possible. Not falsely cheerful or over-bright, but calm and even and, most importantly, strong for me. He looked straight at her and said: 'Mrs Fraser, your son needs you more than ever. You have no choice. You have to be strong for him from this moment on.'

For my mum, these words echoed down the years as she remembered being in A&E with her mother and her then thirteen-year-old-sister, who had collapsed from the pain of an abscess on her brain. The nurse had taken her mother by the shoulders and told her: 'Mrs Wallace, control yourself. You have to be strong.' My grandmother had heeded those words and in that moment of recollection, my mother knew she had only one choice. She asked to be taken to see me *immediately*.

My parents didn't need to be told that they had to be there for me – their love has always been unconditional and constant – but they did need to hear that their strength and positive reaction to me and my situation, from the very first second they saw me, would be one of the key influences in helping me adapt and accept what had happened to me, to shape and frame the coming days, months and years.

That didn't stop the tears as they stood by my bed. 'I'm really sorry, Mum and Dad,' I said, trying to be strong for them. 'I have done the most stupid thing.'

Not missing a beat, my mum said, 'No you haven't, Henry. Whatever this is, we'll get through it together.' With these words, I knew that I wasn't alone and that whatever was going to happen in the following days, I would have my parents by my side. It is difficult to explain how much it meant to hear them say this; the realisation that I wasn't going into the unknown by myself. The giving of support in a time of crisis is surely, above all else, the thing that makes you feel you can face the next minute, and the next, and the moment of hearing them give voice to what had always been there, but which I would now need more than ever, was one of the most important of my life.

Up to that point I had been feeling relatively well. Terrified but physically OK. The only pain I'd felt was when the traction had been put on my head, but ironically for such a serious injury, nothing else. My temperature and blood pressure had been stable and though I was still attached to the weights by my head, I was able to talk. Maybe it was because the adrenaline had been keeping me going, but pretty soon after my parents arrived, my heart rate and oxygen levels dropped rapidly. I was rushed into X-ray again to assess the impact of the traction. Devastatingly, because I was so fit from rugby I had too much muscle in my neck and, since banging my head so hard, these muscles had gone into a tight sort of shock and my neck had not moved, not even by a millimetre. As a consequence of this and my rapidly failing heartbeat, I was taken into the operating theatre where my surgeon opened the front of my neck in a seven-hour attempt to align the vertebrae. This, too, was unsuccessful.

And that is when everything became darker than dark. From the moment I came round from the anaesthetic I knew, within a heartbeat, that my life had changed irreversibly. I was in a completely different state from the day before. Two big tubes were in my mouth and down my throat. I was on a ventilator that was breathing for me. I had another large tube that went up my nose and down into my stomach, through which I was being fed a special liquid supplement as I was unable to eat or drink for quite a while, and I had drips that were feeding me antibiotics intravenously. I didn't know it straight away, but I had contracted MRSA and pneumonia.

If I thought I'd already panicked since hitting my head, I was wrong. I now panicked in the true sense of the word. I was consumed by fear and darkness. I was angry and desperate to get up and walk away. I couldn't move my arms, I couldn't move my hands, and with my mouth and throat now full of tubes, I couldn't make myself understood. And this frantic internal agitation had an acute physical effect. I was starting to having anxiety and panic attacks. This caused my heart rate to drop so dramatically that nothing registered on the screens and it hit zero. Over the course of the next week this happened seven times and I completely blacked out, the monitors screaming and nurses running to my bedside, once brought back to life by the quick action of a nurse punching me in the throat.

My heart was failing and it was failing fast. I was dimly aware that a pacemaker had been wired to my heart in order to regulate my heartbeat. The box was positioned by my head, the ticking ridiculously loud. I was delirious with fever. I was angry and I was frustrated and I wanted to crawl out of my useless body and leave it on the bed.

The next few days were a living nightmare. I was dangerously ill, all options to realign my vertebrae and save my neck from being permanently damaged now suspended as the risk of a further operation was too great. If it hadn't been for my parents, I would have gone to sleep and gladly not woken up. But they kept me going, sitting with me for hours on end, reading to me, asking my help to solve crossword clues and talking, talking, telling me stories and reading out messages from my brothers, my extended family, my mates and their families, and anyone else who knew. We'd worked out a system for me to (try to) get myself understood – they would go through the alphabet and when they got to the right letter, I would make a noise. Then they'd start again for the next letter and so on, and they'd write it down and say the word when it was complete. Good thing we had plenty of time to 'talk'. It took forty-five minutes for me to get them to spell out James Martin as they finished up a quiz on British chefs. I kept quiet when I knew Antony Worrall Thompson was the next answer.

To this day it astonishes me how little my parents revealed the stress and alarm they were going through as they sat by my bed, supporting and loving me. They have since told me – because I've asked – how bleak and terrifying those early days were, alone in a country in which they didn't speak the language, unsure if I would make it through, living from one new horror to the next. They'd had to drop everything, leaving my younger brother in the hands of others, their businesses unattended, and they had to contend with the possibility that life from now on was never going to be the same again. It is testimony to their strength as individuals and as a couple that they were able to get through those days, and remarkable to me how they never cracked. This has taught me so much – that with the love of others, whoever they are, you can face darkness and look through to the other side.

As I came down from the sky-high fevers and the trauma from the first operation subsided, there was one last chance to save my neck, this time by going in through the back. I can still picture the lights on the ceiling as I was wheeled to the operating theatre. The part of the hospital I was in was high-tech and sleek, but the rest of the hospital was still housed in the remains of an old monastery and, as I was taken through the corridors, I thought: *If I wake up and can walk, I will never take anything for granted, ever again.*

The operation was a success in that this time the surgeons managed to realign my neck by screwing and wiring the damaged vertebrae back into place. My neck would be safe from further injury, a crucial factor going forward. When I woke up, though, I couldn't really tell anything had changed and was in much the same state as before, fevered and immobile, unsure of what was going on. It was when my parents had both left the room to talk to the doctor that a nurse, who was checking my vitals, told me that I was never going to be able to move my arms and legs again, and I thought: *What? This is madness.* I couldn't process what he was saying; only that it couldn't possibly be true. Looking back, I must have somehow protected myself from the horror of these words, consigned them to the delirious mass of thoughts that were invading my mind. It was only much, much later that I was able to take these words for what they really meant.

Now that the Portuguese team had fixed my vertebrae, there was little more they could do for me in the short-term and so I only needed to recover enough to be flown home. And I did slowly come out of the fevers and nightmares, the panic and the distress – at times for longer than a few seconds – and when I think back on all the trauma and suffering, there were happy moments, especially when watching a DVD of the 2003 Rugby World Cup Final with my dad. At night, when the ward was quiet and my parents had gone out for something to eat, in my fevered dreams I would be having all kinds of weird hallucinations in the little sleep I had.

2

The little big things

BEING TRANSFERRED FROM Portugal to England was traumatic but I didn't, at the time, realise quite how traumatic. Unknown to my parents or me, by this point not only did I have MRSA and pneumonia, but I had also contracted septicaemia. At first the pilot and medical attendant refused to take me as I was so poorly, but the skilful negotiation of the Portuguese doctors finally persuaded them to fly us home. I was heavily sedated during the journey but that didn't stop me being violently sick and having several panic attacks mid-flight.

Arriving at Stoke Mandeville Hospital in Buckinghamshire, I was put in a side room in the Intensive Therapy Unit (ITU), as far as possible from other patients so as not to infect them. The first thing I remember is waking up in a small dark room, with no windows or natural daylight. I hadn't seen the outside world since I was on the beach two and a half weeks earlier, and I longed for natural light. I was wired up to the usual million machines with tubes going in and out of everywhere. But at least before leaving Portugal I'd had a tracheostomy, which meant that instead of being hooked up to the ventilator by a tube in my mouth, I was connected by a smaller tube through the front of my throat. This meant I could talk a little, though you had to lean in pretty close – practically have your ear to my face – to hear what I was saying. And the ticking of my pacemaker was no longer driving me crazy, as it had been placed under the skin near my collarbone.

Being back in the UK, I desperately wanted to see my brothers. I'd never not been with at least one of them for this long and I needed their strength, the solidness of them by my side. We are fantastically close and fiercely competitive and there is an invisible thread that connects us, wherever we are and whatever we are doing. As I've said, sport is our thing – cricket, swimming, football, you name it – but we have always been rugby mad, inspired by our dad, who played for a local team since before we were born. Having, with some disbelief, produced around a quarter of a team himself, he passed on the love of the real beautiful game to all four of us and, practically as soon as we could walk, we were outside passing, kicking, tackling – a fierce tangle of limbs and tempers. Once we were all old enough, Will and I would take on Tom and Dom in a two-on-two formation, usually in the garden but sometimes on the gravel in front of the house. It would mostly end in an argument and tears but whatever happened the day before got left behind as we hurried out after school to resume our game. And all that scrumming worked – as we got older, we all played for our school, for our local rugby team and at various times represented Hertfordshire, London and the South-East Division.

At the time of my accident, my eldest brother Tom was in his final year at Bournemouth University doing an advertising degree. Will, a professional rugby player, had just come back from rugby training in South Africa for an operation on his ankle and I hadn't seen them or my youngest brother Dom, who was in his first year of GCSE's, for over three weeks. The time had now come.

Up to now I hadn't felt much. The inside of me had shut down. It was weird. It was as though I was there, lying helpless in the bed, but also not there. I was on such strong medication and my body was in such trauma that I was in an altered state, as if I was hallucinating, not seeing clearly what was going on or feeling anything, physically or emotionally. But when my brothers came into the room for the first time, some sort of sense of reality kicked back in and I could see myself in their eyes, my sheer helplessness, and we all broke down together. Just to complete the chorus of tears, my mum and the nurses and doctor joined in. Thinking of it now can make me emotional all over again.

But our tears were not all sad. For a start, we were

together and when I'd been lying face down in the sea, and when my heart had stopped so many times in Portugal, I could have been finished. But here I was: back in England and reunited with my brothers. I was alive and if not kicking, just about in one piece, my heart still beating. It was as if their tears and bear hugs were giving me a massive surge of life and I knew, in those moments, that with my brothers by my side, I would survive this. We had always been – and always would be – a team. I could see how difficult it was for my mum that day, to have brought them to the hospital to see me in this state. But I also saw that now they were on board, they would help see her and my dad through this nightmare.

You can only cry for so long and as I took a good look at my brothers, my tears turned to laughter. I wasn't the only one in trouble. Will was still wearing a great big moon boot from his surgery and it appeared that Dom, too, was not able to walk unaided. Unknown to me, he had cut his foot on a piece of glass and it had become infected, so he was bandaged up, hobbling around on crutches. Ever competitive, we decided that as I couldn't even move, I was definitely the winner on the incapacity front – 'OK, H, you've got this one' – and with this we were able, for now, to dry our tears and revert to our normal banter.

As I listened to my brothers talking, watching Will stroke my foot every few minutes – later he explained that the physio had told Dom to massage his tendons every so often to make sure they were kept flexible, and Will thought that if he could do this to me I might feel something and all would return to normal – I was aware that even at this very deepest dark moment in my life, I could find things funny, drawing strength from those around me. It was brilliant to hear their voices, to watch them around me, every gesture and inflection as familiar to me as this situation was unfamiliar. It made me realise even more how much the support of others was imperative to my fragile life.

From then on, one or more of my brothers came to see me every day, throughout my entire stay in Stoke Mandeville. In the ITU, I wasn't ready or really allowed to see anyone other than family and, because I had MRSA and at times was so unwell with other infections, they had to go through rigorous and lengthy procedures in order to even step into my room –

washing their hands thoroughly, using endless amounts of disgusting smelling hand sanitizer, sometimes even having to wear gloves and face masks. But that didn't stop them. There was a strict limit on visitor numbers throughout the hospital but the doctors and nurses always bent the rules for us where appropriate, letting my brothers in together, even if it meant my parents had to wait their turn in the grim 'family room'.

Despite the presence of my family, the first few days in the ITU weren't easy. For a start, unlike in Portugal where I'd been raised up in a profile bed for much of the day, here I had to lie flat and wasn't allowed to sit up *at all* in case I damaged my neck further. I found this intolerable but what was worse was having to be tilted every few hours to relieve the pressure on my skin. I was strapped into the bed and as it tilted, I would lean slightly one way. In my head that little bit of lean felt like a huge angle, so I was convinced that I was going to fall off. Every time the nurses did it, I'd go into a panic and think, *No, I can't do this*. It took four long days before they agreed I could be transferred but when it came to moving me onto the profile bed, I was terrified. Literally all the nurses had to do was put a board under me and slide me across from one bed to the other, but in my muddled mind this was a massive, traumatic event. There were drugs to calm me down and it was completely worth it as the new bed meant I could see the room, be at eye level with anyone who came in to see me and, at last, watch TV.

The nights were horrible. After the nurses had washed me down and cleaned my teeth, after my dad had said goodnight, as he stayed until late every night, they would put a load of sleeping pills up my feeding tube, but as my mind was running overtime it would work against them. All kinds of weird thoughts and dreams would flash by in what little sleep I could get and throughout the fractured night I would try to focus on the next day, when I would have someone by my side and feel calm enough to nap. Early each morning my mum would arrive and the rest of the family would join her later, staggering their visits so I always had someone with me – Dom would come after school, sometimes doing his homework while I napped, my dad came after work, Will after training, and on weekends Tom would drive up from Bournemouth and we would all be together. I loved that. I also loved that life was carrying on in the outside world for my brothers and I never got fed up of hearing about school, uni, the Saracens, nights out, girlfriends and gossip. They never censored what they told me and I appreciated that – we were never ones to pussyfoot about and now was not the time to start. We watched a lot of TV: endless episodes of *Come Dine With Me* and *The Simpsons*.

I hadn't eaten or drunk a thing since my accident and was still being fed and hydrated through a tube. I hadn't been that hungry so not eating didn't bother me much, but not drinking water was driving me crazy. Because my neck muscles weren't working, there was concern that I might choke and this was not something we could risk. But I went on and on about being thirsty until one afternoon we were given a sponge on a stick that could be dipped in a glass of water and put to my lips so I could suck it. The relief was huge. I realised that I'd never been truly thirsty in my life – water was always within reach, clean and safe – and in this moment of relief, I experienced a lifetime's worth of appreciation for the things I'd always taken for granted. The taste of that first drop of water was so glorious that it made me reflect, if only briefly, on the beauty of life itself. Another new experience that I was adding to all the others. To know something that I hadn't known before meant I could never 'unknow' it and somehow this struck me very forcefully as I quenched my raging thirst with a couple more drops of delicious water.

One Sunday, while I was still in the ITU, my cousins were allowed to come and see me. This was a really big deal, as apart from a very emotional visit from my grandparents, no one else had been permitted to visit. But that morning all my illnesses and infections flared up at once. My timing could not have been worse. I knew I was in a bad way because my teeth started to chatter and, contrary to how cold I felt, my temperature went through the roof and hit my all-time high of forty-one degrees. When my temperature had risen before, there hadn't been great cause for alarm as a fever can be useful in protecting your body against infection, but going to forty-one degrees was dangerous because of the risk to my organs and cells, it can threaten life and often be coma-inducing. My injury meant I couldn't control my body temperature, and I still can't to this day, so whenever I had a fever the only way to keep my body cool was to have bags of ice packed around me. This time I felt really bad, not only from the infections, but also because my cousins had to leave after just a few seconds of being with me. The last thing I wanted was to turn away people who had come to support me and my mind was so fevered and messed up, I took it really hard.

Ordinarily, if my cousins had come to visit, I would have made sure I could spend time with them. I have always valued and enjoyed my extended family and so this feeling of having let them down, when they had travelled so far, of not having been able to pull out all the stops and have them by my bedside, was difficult for me. I felt guilty and, while now I know this was due to the fever and the very early, probably subconscious, realisation that I would have to let go of some of the control and choice I had always exercised, at the time this was a really tough moment. I also knew deep down that they had come to support my parents as much as to see me and that they could still do that, but I wasn't used to letting people down and my thoughts, such as they were, become dark and troubled as I succumbed to the fever.

As the antibiotic kicked in my temperature came down but if it wasn't one thing, it was another, and the day I had my ventilator changed was brutal. I had got used to the huge immobile one wheezing and clunking away in the corner, breathing for me, but in case I needed to transfer rooms I had to be put on a smaller one that could travel with me. To begin with I just couldn't time my breaths with it, convinced it was working against me, which made me panic all over again. It was as if something was blocking my throat, almost as though I was drowning in the sea again. It was horrible and took a while to adjust to, but once it was done I had a new lease of life. Not only could I talk almost normally, it was also one more step towards moving on up to the next ward.

It was then that I was able to see the friends who had been on holiday with me at the time of the accident. Marcus came first and that was a really tearful visit. My mum had picked him up from the station and had tried to prepare him for what he was about to see. But I guess no words really could. My physical mobility hadn't changed since he'd had last seen me on the beach and I was hooked up to a load of machines that were keeping me alive. My friends had been through a lot because of me and it was emotional seeing them again. It wasn't until later, when I was able to talk better and make myself understood and I felt a bit clearer in my mind, that I was able to take in what had happened after I left the beach. I could tell that it still troubled Marcus that he hadn't been able to come in the helicopter with me and that I'd had to go through the first few hours and night alone, but I was able to reassure him that I had been well cared for and my parents had arrived the next day. When I think about it now, my friends had to carry a big burden. We were young and most of us had not had to cope with life-changing events. It was the support of each other, their families, our school and my family that really helped them – another example of how networks of support can be so vital in tough situations. I was also touched to hear of how concerned Marcus and Hugo's Portuguese friends had been and how helpful they were in tracking me down once I had been airlifted off the beach.

My time in the ITU was a real rollercoaster of emotion and physical adjustment. The infections my body had to fight were much more threatening to my survival than we were ever really aware of and, as we were told a long while afterwards, there were times when the doctors were concerned I wasn't going to make it. So, I guess, unknowingly a lot of my energy went into conserving my life. I was also grappling with a range of emotions I hadn't really had to deal with before. Pretty much every time someone came to see me there would be tears at some point and as a typical tough sports-mad guy, I hadn't ever really expressed my emotions so openly. Initially it was difficult and I'd experience some angst and try to stop myself crying but, after a while, it became so truthful and so natural that I stopped minding. Facing the darkness by letting my emotions take me there was hard but cathartic, and something that I am to this day better able to do because of what happened to me.

It was while in the ITU that I became aware of the

cards and messages that had started arriving almost as soon as news of my accident had got out. When I was in Portugal, friends and family had written to my parents at home but now I was in Stoke Mandeville, most of the cards came directly to me at the hospital. At first, while I was still being made to lie flat on my back, I couldn't really take in the sheer volume but, when I was raised up, I was able to see them multiply every day as my family put them up on the shelves, around the walls, anywhere there was a ledge or surface. I was astonished that all these people were thinking of me. And not only thinking of me but also taking time to write, draw pictures and send presents. The effort some people went to humbled me, and each card seemed to build on the emotion of the last.

Nearly every card had a message for me, some words of comfort or hope or love, and I took them all to heart. And the range of people was astounding – from friends and extended family, of course, to friends of friends; teachers, parents and children from my primary and secondary schools, or members of my old rugby teams, some of whom I'd never even known; neighbours and people I'd never met. I hadn't really ever thought about a sense of a tangible community around me before, but the fact that so many people came forward to express their best wishes and supported my parents and brothers was mind-blowing. It made me realise just how kind people are and how, when it comes down to it, we only really have each other in life. To extend friendship, to sustain others during dark times, is the very best of human nature.

I would read and reread and soak up all the positive messages I was receiving. Every hour of every day I would glance at a message or a good wish and I seemed to be feeding my hunger to get better and have hope for the future. It was a card from one of my school friends, that began with a quote from St Francis of Assisi – 'Start by doing what's necessary, then do what's possible and suddenly you are doing the impossible' – which sparked in me a small seed of possibility. Like other friends of mine, he told me he was thinking of me, that he was there for me at the drop of a hat; that he reckoned my strength would see me through. And while this was kind, it was the words of St Francis that really stuck in my mind. I would lie there thinking about what they meant and how they might, in my new condition, apply to me, and they became my mantra during those early emotional days.

And how comforting I found expressions of love or kindness, how refreshing it was to really think about what words meant. Like many, I suspect, I would read birthday cards, or novels and poems set for us at school, and not really pay much attention to the meaning behind the words in front of me. Now, the words were everything and the inspiration I derived from even the simplest of expressions was quite overwhelming. It was the same as I lay in my bed and listened to people talking around me, the words, the silences, the faltering choice of phrases as people first saw me. I learned to listen, to hear what it was my friends, my family, the doctors and nurses were saying and not saying. I even listened to the rhythms of the machines keeping me alive. There was always something to pick up on, always something I could tune into and think about later.

There were so many inspiring words. One of my mum's friends wrote that 'Flesh and blood are what they are in the physical sense but love, courage and passion are the very soul of self.' She told me that she believed life evolved from the inside out. 'Look to who you are inside,' she wrote 'and recognise your achievements throughout these past few weeks.' A bit later down the line, I received a card from the classes I had helped out with in junior school, in which the children had stuck handwritten notes. Their messages were priceless: 'I hope the incident doesn't haunt you for the rest of your life' wrote one boy, while another told me my 'will to live was amazing and to keep on doing good things and never give up!' Writing a card to someone who is unwell is not exactly beyond the limits of most people but to receive those words moved me every single time. They kept on coming and I have saved them all.

And the kindness wasn't confined to me. Food parcels were left in front of our house for weeks on end – proper cooked meals so that my mum didn't have to cook after a long day in the hospital, and so that my brothers and my dad were properly fed before spending the evenings with me. I still wasn't allowed to eat but was pleased everyone else was enjoying the spoils. Sometimes my mum would arrive home and find food, as if it had been conjured out of kindness.

I can honestly say that my soul was saved by these little big things during those dark times. Knowing people were behind me was driving me on, to get as healthy as I could. It was almost as if I had a presence in my mind, of all these people collectively willing me to get better, and I wanted to show them how much their support helped. When I look back, it was undoubtedly the drive to repay this kindness that pro-pelled me to the beginnings of recovery. From the shortest of expressions – wishing you better, thinking of you, hope to see you soon – to longer messages and letters that went into details of people's inner thoughts and prayers for me and my family, to favourite song lyrics or poems that had inspired them through diffi-cult times, to articles about patients who madc miraculous recoveries that people cut out and popped into cards, to presents and parcels, to the delicious food left on our doorstep: it was these things, each and every one of them, that stood one on top of the other, creating a ladder of thoughtfulness that I slowly began to climb.

As my infections began to subside and I got comfortable with my new ventilator, the talk was of moving me from the ITU to the St Andrew acute ward, of getting me off my feeding tube so I could eat again, of working intensively with a physio to free me from the ventilator so I could breathe for myself, even to get me into a wheelchair. The time could not come soon enough.

3

Defeat is Optional

THE FIRST THING I noticed as I was brought into St Andrew was the daylight. As the nurses settled me down and made sure all my machines were working, I couldn't stop looking at the light streaming in through the windows at the far end of the room. Seeing the sky for the first time since my accident four and a half weeks earlier lifted my heart in a way I can't to this day really explain. It was like one step, however small and complicated, closer to being outside.

The second thing I noticed was that there was another person in a bed diagonally opposite mine. Having been in a room by myself – one upside, at least, of having MRSA – I wasn't happy and made this perfectly clear to the nurses, who weren't exactly sympathetic. I calmed down after a few minutes. It wasn't as if we were squeezed into the room – it was, as far as I could see, only the two of us in a four-bed room – but I was by now used to my privacy and didn't really want to be around a stranger 24/7, especially someone who appeared to mirror my situation, helpless in a bed surrounded by machines.

Fortunately, this stranger didn't have the same attitude as me and when the curtains were drawn back, he said hello in such a friendly way that, even though it was difficult to project my voice as far as his bed, I introduced myself. My mum was immediately friendly and interested and over the course of the afternoon, we learned Dan's story: he was twenty-one and had been hit by a car while on his motorbike, coming off with such force that one of his lungs was punctured and his heart literally fell to one side. The doctors had cracked open his ribcage to save his heart and his parents were told to say goodbye at one point, as the impact had been so bad. But the skill of the medical team had saved him and now his heart was back where it belonged. While he would never be able to walk again, he did have the use of his arms. He had also been dogged by infections – the two hundred stitches across his chest had taken ages to heal – and was recovering from an operation on an infected pressure sore, caused from being in bed for so long. He asked about my accident and was so overcome by what had happened to me that I felt horrible for being so selfish in my own thoughts when I'd initially spotted him.

In fact, by the time my dad arrived that evening, fresh air coming in through the open windows – even if the ventilator was still breathing it in for me – the long August day only just beginning to fade, I felt that something had shifted. I recognised this feeling as gratitude – gratitude for the things I had, up to now, taken for granted: fresh air, the sun, the love of those close to me, the hand of friendship offered by strangers. Now, I believe that one of the most mood-enhancing feelings in life is to be grateful for even the smallest of things and, while I was still immobile and unable to breathe or eat unaided, unsure even of my own bladder and bowel movements, helpless in even the simplest tasks, I was hit by what felt like a mountain of gratitude.

And it wasn't just gratitude. I think it was a physical shift too. I have always loved the outdoors, clocking up hours and hours on rugby fields, walking, running, sitting in the garden. But I don't think I had ever really considered the beauty of nature, the texture of the air around me or the significance of sunlight, and the physical jolt of pleasure I derived from fresh air and sunshine that day was something that touched my soul.

As the days in St Andrew took shape, I started to do a lot more with Scott, my physio. I'd been working with him a bit while in the ITU but, now that I wasn't so out of it, our sessions began to get serious. We had clicked immediately and got on really well, his relaxed Aussie outlook chiming with me, his Greek-Cypriot background making him an immediate ally with my mum. Even in my early days in the ITU, he seemed to get me, working gently against my natural impulse not to try something if I was likely to fail. Now, picking up on my sense of possibility, he seized on a growing desire in me to make progress, however small, and to push myself, however slowly. He'd talk to me about the things I could do, never about the things I couldn't, even if at the time I couldn't actually do the things he wanted me to.

However small progress is, it can have a huge impact. When you have to recalibrate even the simplest tasks, such as breathing for yourself or swallowing or coughing, then you have to wipe the slate clean, progressing from where you find yourself. It wasn't helpful to think about my last rugby match, during which I had hurtled through walls of players and sped across a vast expanse of grass. Instead I could appreciate what I had done until now, keep that as a part of me and rather than using the memory negatively – *why can't I do this any more?* – I had to focus on years of building my strength, years of challenging myself, and channel that spirit into the smallest, most basic tasks. This was still very early days, so I wasn't quite there yet, but Scott stirred my desire to step into recovery by concentrating on the tiniest things.

I may have seen sunlight but I still hadn't eaten anything since my accident. Now that I was out of the ITU, the doctors were willing to let me eat, providing I wasn't going to choke. The first step towards this was changing my feeding tube to a much thinner one. It is still surprising to me that with the level of injury I had sustained, relatively minor and fiddly procedures like this caused me so much distress. Taking out the one I had was uncomfortable enough but at least it followed a line from my stomach and up through my throat. Putting the new one up my nose, bending it down my throat and into my stomach, involved a lot of gag-inducing jamming and poking.

A speech and language therapist who specialised in swallowing came to see me to assess my ability to swallow without choking. She gave me half a biscuit and though it was totally weird chewing and crunching and swallowing for myself, I did it. If, at the beginning of the summer, someone had told me that swallowing half a biscuit would have been such a big deal and that such a small thing would have given me so much satisfaction and those around me such delight, I would have laughed at them. But here I was, quietly pleased with this step forward, even if to anyone else it would have been only a tiny, tiny thing.

Eating half a biscuit did not mean I could go straight onto solid food but it did mean we could experiment with bypassing the feeding tube by having puréed food. Being shown a menu was on the same level as seeing daylight again and I took ages choosing my first meal, finally settling on salmon and mashed potatoes, followed by apple crumble. Of all the decisions I had made to get me to this point, choosing salmon was – and remains – by far the worst. Pureed salmon is *disgusting*. It barely got past my lips before I spat it out. It was horrible. And the apple crumble was no better.

Mum could see how disappointed I was, so she suggested to the nurses that she might be able to bring me the food I liked. The following day she came in with jacket potatoes, baked beans and bacon and, once I'd got past the pureed-ness of that, nothing had ever tasted so good. I lived off jacket potatoes and a variety of fillings for days to come, never tiring of the sensation of savouring and swallowing real food. Another tiny step in the scheme of things, but one that made all the difference in the world to me.

After a few days of successfully eating pureed food, my feeding tube was taken out. One less wire coming out of my body felt so good. It also meant I could talk much better – my voice was clearer. Being able to talk so that I could be heard made a real difference to me and made me look forward to visitors even more. Since moving up to St Andrew, a whole lot more people had been coming to see me, so much so that my mum had become my social secretary, picking people up from the nearby station for those who needed it, organising who was coming when.

My schoolmates were amazing: three or four came every single day after school. The journey from Dulwich in south-east London to Stoke Mandeville is around fifty miles and yet there was always a car leaving after lessons or getting the train through London and out the other side. One friend would come a couple of times a week so he could skip sports, saying that his teacher couldn't argue against it. Another came every single Wednesday, without fail, from late morning through to late afternoon. I had visits from some of my teachers – my rugby coach brought me the shirt I should have been wearing in the new season, my form tutor came armed with my AS Level results and when it all got a bit crowded or my schoolmates arrived famished, there was always the macaroni bake that my mum would bring for my friends. Her mum, my *yiayia*, had been hit hard by my accident and did what all Greek grandmas do in the face of adversity: cooked as if my family's life depended on it.

While the afternoons and evenings were busy with visitors, the mornings were spent hard at work. Now that I only had the ventilator and some cannulas attached to me, Scott informed me it was time to start breathing for myself: that now was the time to get serious and apply myself. What he meant by this was a series of steps which, if I persevered and pushed myself, were going to get me off the ventilator and closer to a wheelchair, the rehab ward – and to getting out of hospital.

With all that was happening to me, I realised more and more how much I had always taken for granted and, in my quieter moments, I reflected on this. Breathing wasn't something I had ever even thought about and the idea of being reliant on a machine to do that for me was just about the scariest thing in all this. What if the ventilator failed? I was absolutely determined to come off it so that I could breathe for myself and was totally up for the programme Scott devised for me. I'd already been using a mouthpiece to time my breathing and open up my lungs. Initially this had been tough as my brain had forgotten how to engage with my lungs but, as I was coming to learn, with practise, determination and Scott's encouragement, I could make progress. After a few days on this machine, while breathing into the mouthpiece, he detached me from my ventilator, for a few seconds to start with, then a few minutes, until I could regulate my breathing. As soon as he took off the mouthpiece I had to be hooked back to the ventilator.

Once my breathing action got better, we moved on to using a Cough Assist, a machine that helped me learn how to cough again. Another thing I'd taken for granted – who knew – was the importance of coughing and how essential it is to life, a crucial way of removing mucus from the lungs and reducing the risk of infection. Since my accident, I was getting a lot of gunk in my lungs, all because I was unable to cough it out, and so the next step towards breathing for myself was relearning how to cough. Everything had been stripped back – learning to cough again was something unimaginable a few weeks before. This was a confusing process – knowing when to breathe in when I hadn't taken a breath for myself in so long – and one that took a bit of getting used to. The machine was hooked up to my tracheostomy and then Scott would get into position on the bed, tilt it downwards, climb onto the bed and straddle me, putting his fists under my ribcage as the machine delivered air into my lungs. I'd take a breath in and then as I'd cough out he'd time it and push right up under my ribcage into my diaphragm. It was a case of getting the muscles to remember what they had always done, from the moment of birth up until my accident.

This process was brutal. It wrecked my collar-bones and because of the pressure in my neck, it was horribly painful. But right from the off, there was no question in my mind that I was going to get through it and make that all-important progress. Scott had explained that the longer I could last for on the machine, the nearer I would get to breathing for myself. And as my breathing got better, I began to spend a few minutes a day hooked up to an oxygen tank. Being off the ventilator meant I had to think about breathing, instructing myself to breathe. To begin with, after just a few minutes I had to go back on the ventilator, the effort so exhausting that I would fall asleep straight away.

All this was building up to getting me into a wheel-chair and for this to happen I had to be able to breathe for long enough on the oxygen tank. After what felt like all the physio my collarbones and neck could take, a lot of coughing and breathing on and off the ventilator, these tiny steps forward came together and, when I could manage on the oxygen tank for about forty-five minutes, I was ready. That day my mum and her friend Sandy were with me and it was so good to see Mum's face when we were told I was going to make my first journey out of the ward, sitting upright.

Getting me off the bed and into the wheelchair was a right palaver. I was put into a hoist to lift me out of bed. This was the first time in two and a half months that my legs had been below waist-level and so immediately all the blood rushed to my legs, making me horribly dizzy and not able to see anything, as my eyes were rolling. I was connected to the oxygen tank through my tracheostomy but it was difficult in those initial moments to regulate my breathing and the whole thing felt impossible. But as soon as I was lowered into the wheelchair, one of the nurses held my legs up until everything balanced out and once I had adjusted to this new position, it felt brilliant to be sitting upright. It's amazing how different the world looks when you aren't lying down or tilted up in a bed.

Scott wheeled me out of the ward, showing my mum how to steer me in the wheelchair, avoiding bumps and knocks. They took me to parts of the hospital I had heard about but never seen and Scott pointed out what was what. It was strange to see the life of the hospital going on around me – patients, visitors, the medical staff walking around the place – and it made me realise how much of a cocoon I'd been in. And it was so noisy; every sound was amplified and it took me a while to adjust to being out in this jarring and dazzling new world. Mum had a go at pushing me and while she got used to the weight and movement of the wheelchair and kept driving me into the walls, it reminded me of playing on the bumper cars as a kid and I began to relax and enjoy myself. We went through the bright, sunny café and outside, where the rush of light, that whoosh of fresh air for the first time since the beach, nearly overwhelmed me. I looked up to the sky and down at the lush green grass and I felt myself acclimatising, my adrenaline high. Those few moments outside were like finding an oasis after weeks of aching thirst.

It was as we were coming back in through the big glass front doors of the hospital that, for the first time since leaving the villa for a night out in Portugal, I saw my reflection. But what I saw was not me. Facing me was a razor-thin, weak young man, I had dropped four stone in weight and looked completely lost in a bulky wheelchair. It was not me. His head was tilted back in a support, there was a tube in his throat and an oxygen tank by his side and straps around his middle and his arms were immobile and his legs looked wasted. I tried to look away, to deny what I was seeing, but I knew, in a heartbeat, that this version of me *was* now me. In my mind I was in free fall, tumbling into an unimaginable place.

Somehow I managed to keep it together as Scott pushed me back to St Andrew ward, saying goodbye to my mum's friend and thanking him, but as soon as they'd left and it was just Mum and me, curtained off from Dan, everything hit me. Terrified in a way that I had never before experienced, the magnitude of my helplessness suddenly hit home and I broke down, sobbing 'Why me? Why me?' The reality of the rest of my life was in that reflection and I just didn't know how I was going to go on.

I desperately wanted to hug my mum but I couldn't even do that. For the rest of the day I was inconsolable, sobbing into her shoulder. Up to now my main worries had been around recovering from my infections or getting the feeding tube out or managing without the ventilator for as long as I could. Being isolated from the world in my room, surrounded by family and friends, life had taken on an unreal quality and right in the back of my mind I suppose I had thought that, whatever the severity of my injury, I would, at some future point, be walking out of Stoke Mandeville, my arms and legs reactivated. But seeing myself in those doors – the doors to the outside, to the world I had once walked and run about in – I knew that my paralysis was real and that I was going to be in a wheelchair, my arms as unmoving as my legs, for the rest of my life.

This was my reality but it made no sense. As I was hoisted back into bed, the tears wouldn't stop. When I woke from an exhausted nap, they began all over again. I was still going when my brothers and then my dad arrived, and the depth of my distress must have been really tough for my family as there was nothing that they could do to comfort me. I was staring into an abyss and there was no one there but me. Later in the evening, my dad was reluctant to leave but I wanted to be alone with my thoughts, however overwhelming, and once I'd had my sleeping pills, I convinced him I'd be OK.

Not even my usual heavy dose could send me off that night and I lay awake until the early hours replaying the horror of my reflection over and over again. I was drained from so much emotion – from the high of being in the wheelchair for the first time, to the hours of tears I had cried. My mind was in turmoil and I just couldn't settle. All I kept seeing was the image of me in the wheelchair in those glass doors.

And then, around four in the morning, a strange thing happened. The image didn't seem so terrible. Maybe I'd looked at it so many times, it was becoming normal. Something in my mind turned and a calmness descended, and I had this clarity of thought that there was no point in being sad or angry, that I had no one to blame for what had happened and that I may as well just get on and face what was coming. I'd never had time for self-pity and it wasn't going to become my friend now. I had so much – my family, my friends, a team of people working to get me up and functioning again, and I had made progress, tiny as it was, even since my accident. I had seen the sun; I had breathed in fresh air. And all of a sudden, as if I had been injected with light, I was flooded with a passion for life, a passion for living. As dawn rose, I fell into a deep, peaceful sleep. Tomorrow was a new day.

4

Accept and Adapt

TRAUMATIC AS IT WAS, I really needed a day like that. A day in which all my fears and helplessness were released through my tears, a day in which honesty took over, allowing me to confront the reality of my changing life. From the moment I woke up the next morning, I knew that there was no going back and that I was going to have to be as mentally tough as I could possibly be. As the nurse came to give me my morning wash-down, picking up my arms as though they were weightless, useless things, my resolve took shape and I thought: *I may have lost control of my arm and leg muscles but I haven't lost control of my brain. I can make decisions and I can take control of my situation.*

I have always been competitive and I have always been up for a challenge – years of training and team sports make you that way. I had already been told that I would be in hospital for at least a year and a half, that I would be reliant on a head-controlled chair with armrests for the rest of my life, and that I would be on a ventilator for months to come. Until now I hadn't really been mentally or physically robust enough to take in what that all meant. But, as a fog lifted and the permanence of my disability hit home, I made up my mind to shake things up a bit. I didn't tell anyone; instead, I sharpened my resolve and over the coming days worked just that bit harder, pushing myself that bit further.

I was, by now, managing to spend an increasing amount of time on the oxygen tank but I was still using the ventilator to get me through the night. So, as my new-found clarity clicked into gear, I set myself a goal to go for longer each day on oxygen and into the night without my ventilator. As I had learned, setting myself manageable, realistic goals was the best way to make progress and by building up small increments of time with neither the tank nor the ventilator, I imagined myself off them entirely in the future.

One afternoon, I had a load of mates visiting along with my brothers and, to give Dan some peace and quiet, they took me down to the café, the oxygen tank by my side. Strangely, after about fifteen minutes, I started to get really dizzy and began to feel weird, as though I was losing consciousness. Tom took me back up to the ward, calling over a nurse as we headed for my bed. Seeing the state of me she rushed over and, as she was running through her checks, she noticed that the oxygen tank was off, that it hadn't been switched on the whole time I'd been in the chair. She got me into bed swiftly, ramped up the oxygen and made me wait until I had a couple of tanks inside me. This had been a mistake, of course, and I'd got back upstairs just in time. But I liked the image of myself downstairs in the café breathing entirely for myself, and it made me even more determined to prove the doctors wrong. But it was also a reality check of how serious my situation was.

Eating was now straightforward. I was totally off the pureed mush, my appetite had returned and I was enjoying putting the weight back on and feeling brighter by eating mostly fresh and healthy food. Eating was a big part of my family's life – my mum's Mediterranean background meant a lot of busy, noisy meals around our kitchen table – and until Tom and Will had gone away, the six of us had always eaten together as much as we could, especially at Sunday lunchtime after matches or training. So, when one Sunday we knew that we were all going to be together in the hospital, Mum brought in a home-roasted chicken with her special Greek-style roast potatoes and salad, and we all went down to the café and ate together. It was a brilliant moment – we were in the courtyard of what was then known as 'Jimmy's café' and the sun was shining – and I remember thinking that no matter what had happened and irre-spective of where this table was, being together for a proper meal for the first time since my accident was a truly happy day. We had always been a team –

people used to joke that between my dad and us four boys, we were a mini rugby team – but now I saw it in its reality.

Nothing demonstrated this more than the wordless exchange between them all as they helped me with my hourly 'lean'. Ever since I had been in the wheelchair for more than a few moments, I had to lean forwards for a minute or two every hour to take a bit of pressure off my bum. This was known as 'pressure relief' and was necessary because otherwise the constant pressure of immobility would have led to all sorts of sores and damage to my skin – which, because of the lack of blood flow, would have meant being stuck in bed for ages waiting for it to heal. Having seen the discomfort Dan had been in after he'd had to have a sore operated on, I was clear from the outset that I didn't want this to happen. So, every hour I would ask whoever was with me to lean me forward. My family – and friends – got so used to this that often I didn't even have to ask. Someone would just get up and gently tilt me into position. Knowing that people were there for me and had me and my comfort in mind, without making a big fuss or needing to be asked, made all these new things easier to do.

It was the same with the machine that sat on the table during lunch. Even though I was now eating solid food with no problem, there had been one or two hurdles to jump in order for me to be able to eat away from the ward. My lungs were battered and bruised from the infections I'd had, which meant that my chest was still filling up with rubbish, and at times this interfered with my breathing. For that reason, I had to have a mucus-clearing machine with me whenever I went off the ward. If I needed it, someone would have to take the oxygen off my tracheostomy and feed the machine's tube down into my lungs to suck up whatever gunk was obstructing my airways and lungs. All my family had learned how to use the machine, practising on me at various times, and it meant more than they could know that this enabled us to be together for a couple of hours that Sunday, without depending on any medical staff to see me through. We never really talked about it – they didn't often have to use it, but knowing they could; knowing they had all put time into practising so the burden and responsibility didn't just fall on, say, my mum, and they could all help me if necessary, was enormously comforting. That meal was a milestone and one we will all remember.

※

AFTER ABOUT A month of sharing a room with Dan, we were finally going our separate ways. While I was still carrying MRSA, he had been cleared and now they needed our four-bed room for non-infected patients. Dan went off to a larger ward and I was moved to a small side room. As the days had gone by and we had become a part of each other's lives, I had liked sharing with Dan. He was a calming and positive influence on me and our families got on well. Having my own room again was pretty good, though, and did give my ever-increasing entourage of visitors more freedom to be rowdy, and my brothers and me a chance to watch even more rugby DVDs.

I was sometimes astonished by the number of people that were still coming to see me. There were the regulars – my family, my mates from school – but

now there was also a steady stream from other parts
of my life. Old friends from Berkhamsted School,
local rugby teammates, my brothers' friends, teachers
and coaches going right back to when I was really
young, and my parents' friends and neighbours. I
loved it. I was continually buoyed up by visits and
even if I was tired or having an off day, I liked nothing
better than hearing people talk to each other about
normal, everyday things, however trivial. It kept me
connected to the outside world, to my life before the
accident, and I always appreciated people coming.

To get about the hospital, I was using a wheelchair
with both a headrest and armrests. The armrests had
been a late addition as the chair I'd previously been
using hadn't had them – an oversight and a big
mistake with consequences that remain to this day –
and instead my arms had been placed on a pillow that
sat on my lap. I hadn't really questioned or thought
much about different sorts of chairs but now that I
knew and, I guess, was facing up to the fact that I was
going to be in a wheelchair for the rest of my life, I
figured I should start finding out about the options
available. I'd seen people being wheeled around the

hospital in various chairs but hadn't really taken much notice of their intricacies and the differences between them. A friend of a friend of my parents, a man who had a similar spinal injury to me, had come to show me his chair: I suppose to inspire me. His chair had a headrest that contained touch-sensitive panels and through small movements of his head he could control the TV, turn the lights on and off, and even open and close the electric blind in his room. At the end of one armrest there was a little screen showing what he was selecting with his headrest. He was pleased with all its functions and as he took me through them, I could see the benefits of having some control over my environment.

I wasn't short of offers to view wheelchairs. The wife of a patient in another room on the acute ward popped in one day to ask if I wanted to meet their friend James, who had been injured a few beaches along from me on the Algarve four years before. Despite my focus on making progress, I wasn't yet in the right frame of mind to meet him, so I got Mum to tell her thanks, but no thanks. I thought no more about it, other than how terrible it was that that part of the Algarve had wrecked so many unknowing people. My surgeon in Portugal had told my parents that he operated on at least twelve people a year who were injured by diving into the sea along that coast.

A few days later, I was lying in bed when I saw a guy pushing himself along the corridor outside my room. I worked out that this had to be their visitor and something made me ask Mum to go after him and see if she could talk to him. Mum hot-footed it out of my room and I heard her call after him as he progressed towards the exit. I lay back, something in me stirred by the freedom of those arm movements that allowed him to push himself.

Mum's chat with James turned out to be a pivotal moment and one that I have a lot to be thankful for – another confirmation that focusing on the right things in life is so important. Told he would never be able to push himself, James had been determined to prove his physios wrong and not spend the rest of his life in an electric chair, with head and armrests. While he had more mobility than me and had a little movement in his arms, it was a major feat to be able to wheel himself any distance at all. It was, he told Mum, all, or mostly all, down to Ruth, a very special physio he had come across, who wasn't afraid to fly in the face of perceived wisdom and practice, to listen to her patients and encourage them to push boundaries and get results. In spite of the level of injury he had suffered, the combination of his determination and hard work and Ruth's vision and input, plus a highly developed chair that had a special mechanism in the wheels to aid movement, had resulted in his ability to push himself.

James had shown Mum how his wheelchair worked. Basically, it looked like a normal paraplegic chair but it had power-assisted wheels mounted in place of manual wheels, and a sensor on the outside rim that registered the propelling movement, activating an electric motor in the middle of the wheel. James's physio had enabled him to make the most of the mobility he had and he was now able to push himself around. He knew about me from his friends on the ward and gave Mum Ruth's number as well as his own, inviting me to be in touch as soon as I was ready to talk.

Later, Mum told me that as soon as she got to the

car park, out of earshot of the hospital staff, she had called Ruth from her mobile and, before she had even got into the car, had got her to agree to consider me as a potential client. Ruth practised as an independent physio, having worked for a time at Stoke Mandeville, but no longer came into the hospital to work with patients. This was frustrating but also perversely just what I needed, as it made me want to push myself even harder so I could get off the acute ward and into rehab. I knew that if I was well enough for rehab, I would eventually be allowed home on the weekends and that if I was at home, even for only a few hours, Ruth would be able to start working with me.

Meanwhile, through an even more intense regime with Scott that was making my breathing stronger, I was able to start going to physio sessions in the gym. I could only go at the end of the day, so as not to infect others with MRSA – another advantage of not being able to shake it off. There were only ever one or two other patients down in the gym at this time, which meant I got far more attention than I would have during busier times of the day.

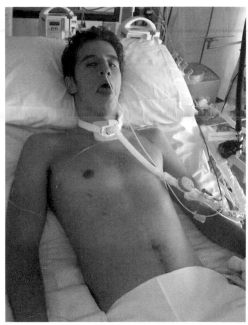

The night before my accident.

About sixty days after my accident. Still with a feeding tube and a ventilator.

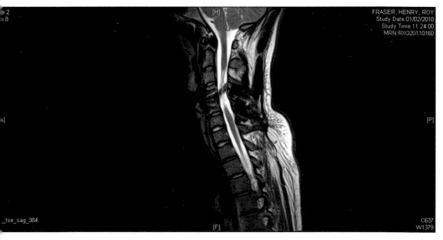

MRI scan of my neck. The short black diagonal line that splits the white and grey lines is where I damaged my spinal cord.

Physio time in the hospital.

The breathing game.

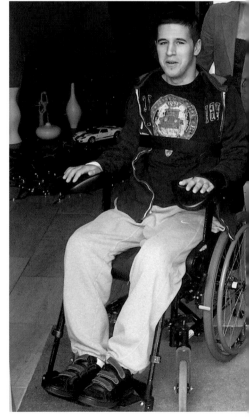

The first day I was allowed to visit home. I still had a chest strap to help me sit up, as well as a high backrest and armrests.

Chilling with mates in hospital.

Exercising with my physio at home, just using my shoulders and tiny, tiny back muscles to pull the weights. I'm always happy when I get to push myself.

Me and my brothers.

A friend's fancy
dress party.
I thought it made
perfect sense
to go as the
Monopoly car.

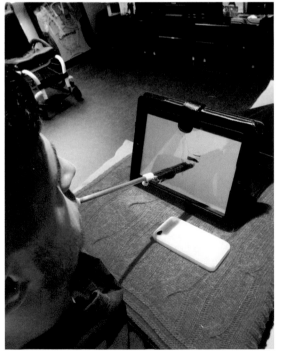

Drawing using my
iPad. This is how
my first works were
created.

Painting 'The Beached Boat'.   Painting 'The King of the Jungle'.

At my first public exhibition in 2016.

With my family after receiving the Blythe Spirit Award at the 2016 Rugby Players Association (RPA) Players' Awards.

Steve McQueen.

Eagle on Black.

The King of the Jungle.

The Beached Boat.

My gym physio, Frances, was great – honest, straightforward and didn't really hold back from telling me what I could and couldn't do at each stage. Being me, I was keen to test the boundaries right from the beginning and while she got the measure of me straight away, pushing me when appropriate, she was never afraid of reining me in. The first thing I did was to sit in what was called a 'passive bike'. My feet were literally strapped in and the pedals moved my legs around, to get some movement back in the joints. My legs had been immobile for almost two months.

While this was happening I was tasked with a breathing game. A stand was put in front of me with a mouthpiece, and I had to wrap my mouth around it; then on a computer screen there was a helicopter that I had to get over various hurdles through my breathing. If I couldn't hold my breath for long enough, the helicopter would come crashing down. Not being someone who liked losing, I would immediately take a huge breath in to get the helicopter to rise, until, inevitably, it fell again. It was a really good exercise and I enjoyed it. Going down to the gym became an important part of my day and I looked forward to it, especially when one or more of my friends or brothers could come with me.

I made good progress and within a couple of weeks there was talk about me coming off the acute ward and going into rehab. Before moving, I had to decide whether to go to one of the adult or paediatric rehab wards. At seventeen, I still had the choice of the children's ward so I went to see both and, while I was surprised that the nurses on each were wooing me to join them, in the end the choice was straightforward. St Andrew had been relatively noisy, with constant buzzing and beeping as patients from the various six- and four-bed rooms called for the nurses. The adult rehab ward felt the same – busy and hectic. And while the paediatric ward felt childish, with its primary-coloured cartoon friezes and shelves of puzzles and toys and Disney DVDs, and I would have fought until my final breath not to be thought of and treated like a child, it was so spacious and quiet and calm – and had its own physiotherapy equipment – that in the end it was a no-brainer.

Once I had made that decision, I set myself a goal, one that even I was unsure was sensible. In order to make full use of the equipment in rehab and get on with my physio, I decided I needed to be off the oxygen tank completely, breathing for myself. I had by now stopped needing the ventilator at night, remaining on oxygen throughout the time I was sleeping. I'd been told when I'd come off the ITU that I'd be reliant on some form of help to breathe for months and months, and now I thought: *No way*. I began to push myself even harder, perhaps too hard – *five-minutes-more-five-minutes-more* was my internal mantra – and one of the nurses who had been observing this gently told me I needed to go more slowly; that it could be counter-productive if my oxygen levels dropped too low and I had to then spend more time on the ventilator to recover.

A week before I was scheduled to move down to rehab, the doctors decided I was breathing well enough to try 'red-dotting' me. Basically, this was where they took me off the oxygen tank and put a red plastic clip on the end of the tube in my throat so that I was connected to nothing and breathing for myself. To begin with this was scary but with Scott's help, I was able to steady myself and breathe. When it became too much for me, the red clip was taken off and I was hooked back onto the oxygen tank, which I have to say was always a relief at first.

But, after a few days of gritty determination, I nailed it. Much to the doctors' amazement, just eight weeks after my accident, I could breathe entirely by myself and was ready to have my tracheostomy removed. I had concentrated on what I could do, not what I couldn't do, and in that way I had made some significant progress.

The day my tracheostomy came out was both the scariest and best day in hospital. As the tube was removed, the doctor asked me if I wanted to have a look at the hole in my neck. Mum held her make-up mirror to my throat as he told me to shut my mouth and breathe through my nose. I was breathing but I could feel the air coming in and out of the hole. The nurse placed a big wodge of gauze over the hole in my neck and it was all over. I was breathing unaided.

That evening, as Dom, Will and my dad arrived, they could tell that something was different but not exactly what. To be fair, it didn't take that long for them to realise I was now, apart from an antibiotic cannula or two, entirely free of tubes and machines. Inside I felt so good because I had set myself a target and I had achieved it. It felt like a victory, flying in the face of the doctors' limited expectations. And victory felt good.

I was ready for rehab and a new goal.

5

Be Grateful

I CAN'T PINPOINT THE exact moment when I became fixated on being able to use my shoulders to push my chair. It may have been when I was finally in a place where thoughts of getting out and going home were becoming a reality. My new ground-floor room was full of light and the floor-to-ceiling window looked out on an entrance-way to the hospital, which meant I could watch people coming and going, and made the outside seem just one step away. It may have been when, in the first meeting with my new consultant on the rehab ward, she stopped a load of medication I'd been taking and then – with what felt like huge belief in me – gave me a discharge date of 10 February. Four months and ten days away, only six months after I entered the hospital and a long, long way off the eighteen months the doctors had originally warned me I would be in for. Before then, she said, if I continued making progress I'd be able to leave the hospital for weekends, with the aim of spending Christmas with my family, at home.

There were only two other patients on the rehab ward, one girl aged fourteen and another aged thirteen, who had suffered spinal cord injuries. One of them – Agnes – had been in a car crash in which her mother had died. Her brother had walked away bruised but in one piece and she had severed her spinal cord. Her dad hadn't been in the car at the time. She had the same level of injury as me and was, understandably, emotionally as well as physically scarred. I felt huge compassion for her and her family, thinking how hard it would be to get through all this without her mother. The other girl, Lauren, was completely crazy, in the best sense of the word – a passionate under-13s footballer who had been scouted by professional teams. She'd been staying with family friends who had a boat moored at the Chichester Boat Marina and one afternoon, when she and her friend were supposed to be cleaning the boat, they abandoned ship, got into a dingy, sailed over to a beach, played a bit of football and then jumped onto a tyre that was attached to a tree and swung about for a while. Always one for exploring, Lauren then decided to climb the tree and it was when she was about fifteen feet up that she fell out. As the tree was overhanging a small cliff, her fall to the beach below was about twenty-five feet in all and she broke her back. She was a paraplegic now. She was able to use her arms, and she was, despite being confined to a wheelchair for the rest of her life, a great force of energy who was fun to be around.

Lauren and I had the same desire to push ourselves and to take a few risks here and there. There was a small playground outside our ward and sometimes when my brothers came, we would get them to wheel us out, put us on the mini roundabout and spin us about as fast as they dared. Lauren managed not to draw any attention to herself, but one afternoon I fell out of my chair while the roundabout was whizzing round, causing the nurses to come crashing out of the ward doors, none too pleased at what had happened. Lauren's desire to get as fit as she could matched mine and she was also in the gym a lot. She is now a professional wheelchair tennis player for Team GB and was the under-18s World Number One for a time.

With just the three of us on the ward, it was quiet, so much more peaceful than the constant coming and going on St Andrew, and as my head began to clear I found myself able to think. The thing that kept coming back to me was the vision of James pushing himself out of St Andrew and I suppose, really, I'd known from the moment I glimpsed him from my bed that if this *could* be done I needed to do it. If I'm totally honest, for me, going into an electric chair with head and arm support for the rest of my life felt like giving up. I knew I could do more and while I didn't have the small amount of mobility James had in his arms, I did have a very very small amount of movement and feeling in the top of my shoulders, movement that with the right exercises could work in my favour.

As the old saying goes, you can't run before you can walk, so for the time being I had to focus on what was achievable and work at building up my strength. Being in a gym was familiar territory and if there is one thing I know, it's the value and addictive appeal of exercise. Before my accident, I loved nothing better than a good gym session, lifting weights, running, working on specific parts of my body. In rugby training sessions I always paid a lot of attention to the theory behind particular exercises and, as I have a visual sort of brain, had a clear understanding of which muscles do what and which exercises are good for particular muscles.

When you have a spinal cord injury, even one as severe as mine, exercise is incredibly important, doing all the things it does for anyone: slowing down the rate of bone loss, improving the immune system, reducing the risk of diabetes and heart disease, helping healthy bowel activity. I had to recalibrate, but with guidance from my physio, there were days when

I was getting a good workout that left me exhausted in that satisfying exercised-out sort of way.

In itself, being on the rehab ward meant I could do more complex and useful exercising and a whole raft of equipment and techniques suddenly opened up to me. On one side of the gym was a massive railing system that I could now use to exercise my shoulders. Frances would put my arms into ropes with elbow- and hand-holders that kept my arms elevated, and she'd encourage me to use my shoulder muscles by helping me swing my arms about. It was really hard at first but through visualisation and intense concentration I was able to pinpoint the relevant muscles and drill down on focusing all my effort into working them.

I was no longer reliant on being in the gym to exercise. The ward was well equipped and I had almost all-day access to a particular bike that became a favourite of mine. The Functional Electrical Stimulation bike, or FES for short, was a totally different thing to the passive bike I'd been strapped to while on the acute ward. This more sophisticated machine provided my muscles with a true workout, stimulating the lower motor neurons that were connected to my spinal cord. Mum quickly became good at setting me up — connecting pads from the bike to my hamstrings, glutes and thighs, which then worked my muscles in such a way that they were moving the bike, rather than the bike moving them. It was brilliant for blood flow and for releasing hormones round my body, and over the days and weeks that I used it – often I would cycle twelve miles a day – my balance and posture improved and saved me from pressure sores, as my skin felt elastic and healthy again. And, of course, it became addictive: the more I was on it, the more I wanted to do and the more I wanted to do, the closer I was to starting work with Ruth.

If I had any chance of being able to spend my life in a wheelchair without a full back or head support, I had to be able to balance and remain upright for long periods of time, and this meant rigorous exercising of my back. In order to do this, I would be lowered onto the edge of a bench and a physio would hold me from behind, their arms around my chest or on my shoulders, while another physio would bring my elbows onto a table in front of me, holding them in place. The physio behind me would lean me forwards, allowing me to take the weight through my elbows, and get me to think about pushing down through one and then the other, over and over again, with the aim of moving them from side to side. This was the most physically shattering thing I did the entire time I was in hospital, but my back muscles were definitely getting stronger.

There is no doubt that the physio the hospital provided was helpful and I was giving it my all – and some – but what frustrated me were the limitations that I felt were being imposed on me. Collectively, it seemed that the hospital took a conservative and reluctant approach to anything different and had little vision of me in anything but the wheelchair they deemed suitable for a patient with my level of injury. Protocol says that someone with zero arm and leg movement should be in a head-controlled electric chair, but I knew I could do something different. Sometimes I felt that if I could have channelled all the energy that I had to use to push against the system into pushing my chair instead, I would have got to Timbuktu and back.

As well as doing physio, I was also seen by occupational therapists whose job was to prepare me for 'readjustment' – getting back to a 'normal' life living with my disability. This was a less active form of adjustment and to be honest I wasn't always that up for it. Often I was not the most receptive of patients – not because I didn't want to know, but because it seemed somehow so *inactive*. I didn't mind the physical aspects, like the work they did on my wrists and hands, bending the bones and trying to maintain flexibility, but at the time, all the ins and outs of hygiene, bladder function and bits of equipment didn't always hold my attention. The group classes I was supposed to attend were also a bit of a drag – people coming in to talk 'at' us about their experiences or life in a wheelchair. Occasionally there would be a talk that would resonate with me – either shock me or make me see things differently. The one on sores and skincare really hit home when we were shown gruesome photos of wheelchair users who'd insisted on wearing such tight jeans that the skin around their groin and upper thighs had literally worn away.

I also wasn't a great fan of the counselling sessions

I was offered. I know the counsellor was just doing her job, but to me it felt as if she was digging around for stuff that wasn't there. One of the best battles I fought during my time at Stoke Mandeville was when one of the nurses tried to force me into having more sessions with the counsellor, telling me that I hadn't fully accepted my situation, that I was always pushing back against them, wanting to be in a different chair, wanting to do the things that the books said I couldn't do, pushing myself in a way that couldn't get me to the places I wanted to go. But I didn't need those sessions precisely because I had accepted my situation. I knew exactly where I was. I simply wanted to do more than I was told I could do.

This sharp mental resolve was new to me. Before my accident I'd been physically strong but mentally weak, scared of trying new things or going outside my comfort zone for fear of failing, but now my strength had to be in my head. Yes, I was busy trying to prove that I could still do things with my body, but the strength for this had to come from within, from an inner strength of mind. I was coming to see my life before the accident with some perspective, how I had taken so much for granted and how I could have done so much more while I had the use of my arms and legs. But rather than dwell on what I couldn't do, I could see that I now had the opportunity to do more. I was determined to achieve my goals, however big or small, not only for myself but also to show my family, my friends, my school and all the people who had been giving me such incredible support, that I was worthy of their time and attention.

The 'discussion' with that nurse fired me up and I put even more effort into my physio sessions. It was a few days afterwards that I was told I could go home for the weekend. This was brilliant news but I was fully aware that while I had the luxury of lying back and anticipating the pleasure of being at home, there was an awful lot of preparation going on behind the scenes so it could happen. Caring for me was now a full-time job and without the nurses and doctors and support staff at the end of a buzzer, the burden was to be my family's.

Not that they seemed to see it that way. Ever since my new consultant had mentioned the possibility of me coming home for a weekend Mum had been busy liaising with the hospital and the local council, preparing our house with the right equipment, supplies and medication, and getting used to driving the specially adapted 'Barbara bus' that she would be loaned to transport me to and from the hospital. A bed on wheels had been secured and, most importantly of all, the thing I had been working towards: my first appointment with Ruth.

Coming home was amazing. My mum had made a 'Welcome Home' sign out of colourful wallpaper from the sample books she uses for her work, and my dad and brothers were all waiting. It was pretty emotional when they wheeled me through the front door. Actually being there, I realised how much time I'd spent imagining the rooms, the light, the space and colour of my home, how much I had thought about sitting around the kitchen table with my family or watching rugby on TV with my brothers, but nothing really prepared me for the reality of being back – the warmth and comfort of the place where I had always lived – and for the first time I really understood the true sentiment of coming home.

After a tearful welcome and tour around the downstairs – it was weird to think I wouldn't be going upstairs to my bedroom any time soon – where I was shown my new sleeping arrangements, under the window in a corner of the kitchen for my first night at home; Ruth arrived. Five-foot, sixty-year-old, plain-talking, no-nonsense Ruth; who, from the very first question – 'Well, Henry, what is it you want to be able to do?' – set about helping me achieve my vision of pushing myself out of the hospital. Not for one moment did she question my ambition and we soon came to see what James had meant about her unlimited horizons. I was so used to the hospital's 'by the book' way of looking at things – if you had this level of injury you could only do A and B, not C and never, ever D – that when she turned that upside down: 'Henry, if you can do A and B but can't do C, it doesn't mean you can't do D, E and F,' I knew she was the right person for me. I'd come so far in the weeks since my accident; now not minding if I tried something and it didn't work. If that happened, I made myself draw a line under it and either resolve to come back to it another time or move on.

Right from the start Ruth involved my family,

showing them what they could do for and with me. One of the best things she did that first day was to show Tom and Will – Dom was too small back then and my dad had a bad back – how to do a 'standing transfer' so that I could come out of my chair and lie on the sofa. Basically, one of them had to stand in front of me, straddle my thighs, put their arms under my armpits, lock their hands around my back, grab me, pull me in close, stand up with a straight back and bring me up with them. Her instructions were so clear, so matter-of-fact: '*Pull* him, Will! He isn't made of glass!' that you couldn't help but follow them, apply them and never have to ask again.

She showed us new and different exercises that I could do while lying in bed or on the sofa and she had all these little tricks of the trade. She was the Mary Poppins of the physio world, making everything seem effortless, grounded and doable.

I returned to the rehab ward full of home-cooked meals (my grandparents had piled in with heaps of food, in addition to my mum's cooking) and hope and an even greater sense of determination to wheel myself out of the hospital. Because the physios had their way of doing things and I wasn't supposed to be using private help, I didn't tell them about Ruth, but there was no disguising the fact that after each subsequent weekend at home, I would return to the hospital full of new ideas as to how to do my exercises, and within a few weeks I was able to go from a chair with a headrest to a smaller chair with no headrest. This was, even by my reckoning, a massive step forward and one that made a huge difference to the way I saw myself.

Once the headrest came off – 'Well *done*, Henry!' – Ruth told me to ask for a chair with special wheels that have handles on the rims, little knobs that help those with small amounts of hand movement to practise pushing. The hospital supplied this, but asking for it made the physios even more suspicious as I had no movement in my hands and, if they hadn't realised already, this was when they got it firmly in mind that I must be working with someone else outside the hospital. The next time I saw Ruth, she showed me a letter from the senior physio at the hospital that suggested in no uncertain terms that she stop seeing me. As if. She tossed the letter aside, took hold of my arms and put my hands on the back knobs. She made me think about pulling and I closed my eyes and with all the mental energy I could summon, I concentrated my mind on engaging my trap muscles, my chest and my lats, places I couldn't feel, to push down into the wheels. It took a fair few goes and because I had such little use of any of these muscles, it was mostly a force of mental will, but eventually it worked. Though the movement was tiny, imperceptible even, to begin with – it would have taken me about ten years to push myself from my hospital room to the car at that rate – every fraction of movement felt like a mile of possibility to me. I spent hours – literally hours – practising at home, going as far as I could in the kitchen and living room, the mental and physical strain both shattering and exhilarating.

This seemed to mark a turning point and when the hospital physios could see how hard I was working to push down on the wheels, how determined I was to achieve movement, without saying anything explicitly they started to really work with me, building on what I achieved each weekend. I was given an even smaller chair – an ordinary wheelchair – with just a slightly higher back to help me keep my balance. No one with my level of injury, they told me, had ever been in a chair like that before.

Ruth seemed to think I was ready to try the E-motion wheels that James had been using, so when the rep from a wheelchair company came round to see me – it was always surprising to me that there was so much *on sale* to the patients – we asked if he could bring one of those to the hospital. It gave me a sense of independence as, once the remote control round my neck had been switched on, and someone helped me put on gloves that had splints in them to keep my hands stiff, with fingerless leather gloves over those to help me adhere better to the wheels, I would force all my concentration into my shoulders and, with a great deal of effort, get moving. And once I got going, I couldn't stop and would practise as much as I could, up and down the ward, in and out of the lobby. People would come from all over the hospital to watch. And it felt great. I was now even closer to achieving my ultimate hospital goal and I was in serious training mode.

Seeing how comfortable and happy I was in this

chair, my parents arranged to buy a demo model from the wheelchair suppliers. Since my accident, a trust had been set up for me and thanks to the generosity of friends, family and fundraising activities at Dulwich College and Berkhamsted School, there was some money waiting for me to use on equipment and private physio. I've always been humbled by the support and love shown to me and, when these things became as tangible as a wheelchair that was going to make all the difference, I was overwhelmed with gratitude. As soon as I knew that no one was going to take the chair away from me or try to put me in an unsuitable one, I felt secure and ready.

The week before I left was weird. I was excited about going home but also worried about what it would be like without the support I was so used to in the hospital. What was going to happen if things went wrong or my family couldn't cope? I did have some dark moments of doubt and crises of confidence. But that was mostly at night as I drifted off to sleep. During the day I focused more than ever on pushing myself around. There were several meetings with doctors, nurses and the occupational therapists, where we went over my drug regime, the amount of equipment supplied by the local council that I would need, and hygiene routines. They gave us loads of extra stuff, especially leg bags for my urine, and each day my family would empty my room a bit more, taking down the cards, drawings and photos that still adorned the walls and shelves, packing up my clothes, DVDs and stuff I had somehow managed to accumulate.

And then came the day itself. After six months of being in hospital, I was free to go. I hadn't been emotional for a while and even on that final day I wasn't, as the main thing was to show everyone that I could push myself out – from my bed to the car park, a distance I would have managed in a couple of minutes six months before but which now felt like miles and miles. As I sat in the chair, my hands on the wheels, the nurses stood on either side of the ward and made a tunnel for me to drive through. There had already been a lot of hugging and crying in the days before – my mum in particular had got extremely close to the staff – and there were a lot of tears as I began my journey. Down through the tunnel, out into the lobby, through the exit doors, and on to the car park. Will and Dom were waiting for me by the car and as I drove my shoulders down as hard as I could, with no arm movement or arm control I pushed myself out into the light, towards my smiling brothers.

I'd done it.

6

Pushing Myself

I'D PUSHED MYSELF out of hospital and now I was home. Being back for good took a bit of getting used to, especially my reliance on the outside carers who, alongside my family, I was dependent upon in one way or another 24/7. Again, the positive and cohesive way in which they all set about caring for me – which crucially also meant giving me my space and voice to determine my own needs – further emphasised the importance of teamwork and our collective, largely unspoken attitude of always looking forward.

If I do look back, and at that time in particular, I realise how much stronger mentally and emotionally I'd become. While Mum, Dad and my brothers had more or less always had a glass-half-full outlook on life, I'd been a worrier, cautious and careful in practically everything I did. I felt that as much as they helped me, I helped them with my new-found resilience. They also fed off me. Since my accident and in a relatively short space of time I'd become far more resolute, far less frightened of trying new things even if they didn't work out, and had somehow rewired my brain to avoid looking at the wrong things. Instead, more often than not, I was able to look to the right things, the places where my energies would be rewarded by progress, however small. All of us had come to realise that we would become stronger if we focused on the things we were able to do, not the things we couldn't. And for me, most signifi- cantly, I'd come to see that it is the art of striving that gives life meaning, that the greater the challenge ahead of me, the more alive I felt; that the greater the challenge, the greater the opportunity to achieve my goals, and the greater the goals, the better I could become.

I wanted to harness this new-found attitude to life and focus on my next set of goals. I understood clearly, perhaps more clearly than anything I'd ever understood in my life, that I needed to keep well and get as fit as I could be. Being physically strong, whatever my limitations, would contribute to staying mentally robust, and vice versa. So for the next few months I concentrated on my sessions with Ruth, who now came two or three times a week, working with me in new and intensive ways. I loved it – being in control of my body through her expert guidance, discovering new exercises I could do to strengthen my back even though I couldn't feel it, just focusing with my mind so I could remain in my unsupported wheelchair – and when she wasn't there I spent hours on the FES bike that we'd bought with the money that people had so miraculously raised and made available to me.

This period wasn't without its challenges. I was exacting and demanding, possibly even a bit OCD in my instructions to have my arms placed just so on the cushions on my lap, or to have a specific song playing while I was doing a particular exercise. Just as I was overwhelmed with gratitude the moment I saw daylight for the first time since my accident, I was thankful all over again for something, every single day. And my soul was still being saved by those little big things that kept happening – a kind word, a helpful gesture, friends messaging, the never-ending support of my mum and dad's friends. When people bear you in mind, the obstacles become easier to face.

After these early few weeks of adjustment, getting into some sort of routine, my mind settled down and I began to think of my next big challenge, a challenge that would move my life on. Just thinking about it got my brain whirring and my heart racing and when I was on the bike, I gave it shape and form and decided to talk to my parents about seeing it through.

Even though I hadn't exactly been Einstein at school, I'd been a good and conscientious student. I'd done well enough in my GCSEs and things were still unfinished. I'd done my AS Levels and wanted to complete the task and get my A Levels. I've never been good at leaving things half done; my childhood was dominated by hours and hours finishing complex Lego constructions that would hold my family up for ages. The idea of going back to school had been swirling around inside me for some time before I even left hospital and, when I told my parents that I wanted to complete the final year, they were surprised but totally supportive. So began a few months of discussion with the powers that be at Dulwich, and a look into what might be possible.

There was nothing wrong with my mind and since that's what I'd be using to study, it seemed, to me anyway, doable to go back to school. I didn't want to approach this half-heartedly and I didn't want to change to a local school. I wanted to go back to Dulwich as a weekly boarder, attend classes like everyone else, and have as normal a life as possible while there.

Dulwich College is a visionary place where things happen and, thanks to the enlightened and unconditional co-operation of the teachers and staff, it appeared to be entirely possible for me to go back. They did everything they could to get me back to school. They showed incredible support from the very early days of my accident. And so, at the start of the academic year, I returned to school to do my A Levels: I chose PE and economics. We decided between us and the school that a full week might be too much for me, so a shorter week – Sunday night to Thursday afternoon – would be better. I had a carer boarding with me to help with my daily routines and, generously, we'd been given the entire ground floor of one of the boarding houses to ourselves. We had a room each and the school adapted and kitted mine out, installing a special shower chair in the bathroom and loads of heaters to keep me warm for when my body was unaware it was cold.

My parents were apprehensive as to how I would meet this new challenge. So was I, and it took a while to settle. My room was pleasant enough but this wasn't home, with its familiar light and comfort. And while I had my carer and support from the staff, I was largely on my own, without the quiet and constant security of having my mum around. I was also aware of the physical and emotional toll that a new environment and routine might take on me. Getting up each day at quarter to six and going to bed around eleven

– with a busy day in between – was shattering, and in the first few weeks it took a lot of determination and will to power on through. Full school uniform – shirt, blazer, smart trousers and tie – wasn't exactly my outfit of comfort; nor was having to get into it the best start to the day. Overcoming one of my biggest hates – not doing my top button up – became a huge deal and a couple of times nearly derailed me. Because my neck was so much bigger and out of proportion to the rest of my body, muscled and broad, I couldn't find a shirt that would do up around it, and that really bugged me. It's strange sometimes how the smallest things assume the greatest proportion. You'd think I'd have had more pressing concerns.

At least I was allowed to miss registration as it took me so long to get ready each morning. I was also fortunate that my lessons had mostly been timetabled to begin mid-morning so I never had to be in class first thing. The school had moved my PE class so that it was near my economics classroom, which cut down on the distance I had to travel between periods and being part of that bustle when everyone tips out of one lesson and hurries to the next. They also let me take naps when I needed, though I was absolutely determined in my own mind never to sleep during any of my classes.

Two A Levels isn't exactly a packed timetable and I made sure I paced myself so I could get to each lesson. But there were so many calm and unobtrusive ways in which the school supported me, things they'd thought of and put into action without me or my parents having to even ask, that I never once felt I was a burden to anyone. If I couldn't get an assignment in on time, none of my teachers minded, though I wasn't given any concessions when it came to marking my sometimes scrambled essays, which I'd do at home at the weekend using my voice-recognition equipment. And there were acts of kindness that made me feel looked after, especially Matron stashing my favourite chocolates in my desk drawer, or the tutors who looked after my boarding house coming in for a chat at the end of the day to catch up and see how I was getting on.

While I was at school for most of the week I couldn't see Ruth, so my physio sessions went right down, and this was hard for me. But I'd become resourceful, more easily able to see around problems to find solutions. I bought a 'rolling road', a compact sloping ramp with rollers that my carer would assemble, push me up onto, and then leave me on for a couple of hours while I worked out, pushing down into my shoulders and moving the wheels at various speeds depending on how tired I was. If my friends or tutors came into my room after prep for a chat, they would often find me working out, trying to keep my muscle tone tight and ready for sessions with Ruth back at home. I clocked up miles each week, happy in my new comfort zone of pushing myself.

Just as well, as I'd piled on the weight since coming back to school. Mrs Maguire's chocolates were definitely a part of it but I was also eating three pretty big meals a day: a boys' school hot on calorific food. I needed the fuel to keep myself going but it wasn't until I finished school that I caught sight of myself in a mirror and was shocked that I looked fat. I'd always been trim and fit and in my new-found state of resolve, I vowed to change my eating habits. To this day, I'm extremely careful with what I eat, generally missing out on a big meal in the middle of the day as this tends to make me feel lethargic and useless in the afternoon.

Obviously I couldn't take notes or even use a computer in class and the school suggested that I have someone 'scribe' for me, so we advertised and found Hayley, a psychology graduate, with whom I clicked immediately. She was fun and super-organised and got on really well with everyone. It was brilliant having her by my side in class, taking notes. She hadn't studied PE or economics but by the end of the year she could have taken the exams herself as she'd really got into the subjects. She was so quick and bright that we'd have some great discussions on some of the trickier topics, which really helped me out.

The PE A Level has a physical component, which I couldn't do, so to get around this one of my teachers proposed to the exam board that, given my circumstances, I do a project that had a practical side to it. He then came up with the idea of me analysing a series of rugby games from DVDs, using the new technology that premier league rugby clubs had pioneered to examine tactics, knock-ons, forward passes and the like, and he arranged for this guy to come in and show me – and, of course, Hayley, as she would be the one actually inputting data – how to use it. This was the part of my work that I enjoyed the most and Hayley soon became an expert in yet another field she'd known nothing about before she met me.

My friends had all left school by now – I'd been in hospital and at home for much of their A Level year – but one of my friends, Ollie, who'd been at the school on a rugby exchange from Cape Town for one term during my AS Level year, had moved over full-time to do his A Levels. I was so pleased he was there and soon we spent most of our free time together, picking up where we'd left off when he'd returned to South Africa. I knew a few of the boys from the year below and often my mates who hadn't yet gone on their gap-years or were down from uni would come by and see me. Those who were away were always in touch, checking up on how I was getting on, nostalgic, even just a few months out, about school life. A couple of my friends were working at the school in their gap years, helping with junior classes or sports coaching, and would always come and spend time with me.

School isn't only about studying and learning: the social side is just as important and while, most days, I only had a little triangle to navigate – from my room to the sixth-form block to the dining room – I often came into contact with boys from other years. It was amazing how normally I was treated, though initially some of the younger boys were a bit shy in approaching me. But as I became part of the fabric of school life and they could see I was able to talk and join in with things, they'd come up and say hi, and that really made my day.

While I was happy and managing well at school, the physical fallout was massive. The fatigue was like nothing I'd ever experienced, building to such a crescendo each week that the moment I got in the car with Mum on a Thursday afternoon I'd fall asleep, waking up three or four hours later still in the car on our driveway, too fast asleep for my mum and carer to have moved me into the house. I was determined to stick to my weekly sessions with Ruth, which was Friday taken care of, so weekends were the only time to chill and recover. It was only thirteen months after my accident and I wasn't really aware of the extra rest my body still needed. I was mostly tired and often ill with urine infections, missing a good fifteen weeks of school throughout that year.

But I did it. In June I sat my exams just like everyone else, with the same stress and nerves. Hayley wasn't allowed to scribe for me because she'd been in all my lessons and could have written better answers than I was capable of, so a teacher wrote for me. I got loads of extra time and I literally dictated my answers to her. I talked for about sixteen pages' worth in my economics exam. Once I was on a roll I couldn't seem to stop, regurgitating all I'd learned in what I hoped was a reasonably focused way. It's weird saying answers out loud: you lose the self-awareness that comes with writing and the small corrections you can make immediately. At first I couldn't help but try to read the teacher's body language – maybe she'd stiffen or stare questioningly when I got something wrong or was being clumsy in my response – but soon I was in my stride, concentrating on bringing some degree of coherence to what I was saying. Economics was tough – all those theories were hard enough to keep straight in my mind, let alone speak about – but I'd found the subject so interesting and engaging that I was able to give reasonably good answers.

Having achieved what I'd set out to do, leaving school was an opportunity for me to take stock, stronger in myself for focusing on the things I could do, making progress, completing my school days just like everyone else who'd stayed to do A Levels. And even though I'd been ill more regularly than I'd thought possible, causing worry and grief for my family, going back to school had been the right decision and I left with a great deal of dignity and an immeasurable amount of gratitude.

Being home again meant yet another period of adjustment but this time I felt hugely more independent, or rather, less dependent. It wasn't only me that had to adjust. My parents had been able to pick up the pieces of their lives while I'd been at school, secure in knowing I was in a safe and caring place, and now here I was, back, with all my daily demands, in what I now see was a state of physical depletion. For the better part of the next year, I concentrated on building myself back up, doing physio with Ruth up to three times a week. And it worked – after a few months

I was in the best shape I'd been since my accident and could do two hundred reps of some exercises. I felt healthy and well again, less tired, more alive in the moment and, of course, I now needed a new challenge.

When I'd first come home from hospital, I'd set up a website, using voice-recognition technology, so that all those who'd contributed – and were still contributing – to my recovery could see how I was getting on and how much their generosity was fuelling my progress. At school the teachers had found it useful in prepping the younger boys about my accident, as I'd also written about what had happened to me. I hadn't kept it up that much – I'm not a natural writer – but now I had some time on my hands, I revisited it and wrote the next part of my story. I was using my iPad by this point; I'd received it at Christmas during my time at school.

I clearly wasn't too bad at it as I was approached by a couple of guys my brothers and I knew to contribute to their rugby website. They wanted me to interview and analyse the players coming up through the school and university rugby teams, and comment on improvements that could be made for young players. I was apprehensive about the quality of my writing but, as the subject matter was essentially a lot of what my brothers and I talked about, I could make my articles conversational, if not exactly literary.

It's amazing what pushing yourself in areas outside your comfort zone can do. I'd been worried that, having finished school and devoted time to getting myself into better shape, there would be a huge void and I wouldn't know how to fill it. But I was learning that taking opportunities as they arose, even if they felt a bit too challenging, made life interesting. When I got a call from Will's agent, who had seen and liked the stuff I was writing, asking if he could approach ESPN to see if they wanted to use me, I didn't even hesitate to accept. I was on a roll, as writing for the ESPN website led to some of my stuff being taken by Sky, and that led to the CEO of Saracens offering me a three-day-a-week job. Basically, I had to do pre-match stuff for their website, writing about the teams they were playing, getting stats about them, doing – mostly by email – interviews with the players.

Earning money gave me some feeling of independence and worth. I'd always thought I'd have been heading to uni after A Levels but the situation I was in had allowed me to look at different options, and here I was earning money and doing something I could really only have dreamed of. If I couldn't play rugby any more, the next best thing was surely being paid to write about what had always been my passion.

The CEO at Saracens, Edward Griffiths, had me under his watch and one day asked me if I'd ever thought about public speaking. That silenced me for a moment or two. If I'd thought writing was beyond me, then public speaking was on another level. I had always hated speaking in public, I couldn't even talk in front of my classmates giving a presentation. It was something I'd certainly thought about in the sense that I admired those of my mates who'd debated and spoken in public. I'd never had the confidence to do it myself but, after a brief hesitation, this new me found myself replying that, yes, I had thought about it but had never got round to doing it. Edward immediately offered to invest in a colleague of his to coach me and before I knew it, I was working with David Priestley, a psychologist by training, taking everything off my website, condensing all I'd written, squeezing it down so that any talk I gave wouldn't last more than half an hour. It was a real skill, the way he worked; managing to retain the details of what had happened while also bringing out the most important things I'd learned along the way. When you're so close to your own life, especially when something has turned you upside down, it's hard to stand back and see, beyond the incident itself, which bits, if any, are interesting. Why would anyone who didn't know me be the least bit engaged – beyond the shock value – by what had happened to me? It wasn't as if everyone leapt into the sea on a daily basis and my story would warn them not to. I wasn't famous, I wasn't insightful, I hadn't done anything impressive. And it was dead important to me not to make any talk I was going to give feel sentimental or self-pitying – that just wasn't ever and still isn't me – but, on the other hand, how could I ever talk about my experience without mentioning the unconditional love and support of my family, the kindness of others, all those little big things that had made our lives so much easier? We had our work cut out.

After a few sessions, David said that he was going to set a date 'the following April 2014' for my first talk and as 'the following April' seemed miles off, I said that was fine, as if I never thought that time would come. But then it was March and suddenly one of my worst nightmares was about to come true. The week before the talk, David took me to speak to six people who worked at Saracens for a practice run and, while that was useful, I couldn't stop thinking of the fifty or so people – players from the Saracens first team and staff, including members of the board – that I'd be talking to for real in a few days. The whole week before the talk I was a wreck, lost inside my mind, terrified that everything would go wrong and the audience would peel off one by one, leaving me alone in my wheelchair facing an empty room. Maybe, I thought, as I woke up from yet another nightmare, this really was one challenge too far.

On the day itself, I was with Will and a couple of the other players while they ate lunch. I was too nervous to eat anything. My teeth were chattering and I could barely speak. David took me into the room before everyone else assembled and he made sure I could see that all the technical things were working – the overhead projector, the laptop that he'd be using to scroll through my talk as I gave it. It was a beautiful day and the sun was streaming through the windows and, as I was introduced and everyone clapped, I could see that their faces were in shadow and the sun was preventing me from seeing if they were looking directly at me. This helped me so much that it was as if nature was on my side. The room was wide and I could look around a lot, which also made it easier. As silence fell, the room filled with a kind of expectancy and I told myself: *Don't let yourself down, tell them what you want them to hear.* David smiled at me and I began to speak.

One line in and I was away. Perhaps I had been waiting to tell my story all along, perhaps somewhere I wanted to share what I had been through and make it easier for others to see that I was OK, despite being a tetraplegic, the worst nightmare possible for a team of professional rugby players. When I finished and the audience clapped it was the biggest relief in the world. I suddenly felt a foot taller, as if I could sit up straight and look them in the eye, and

I was quite overwhelmed as people came forward to congratulate me.

Since then I haven't looked back and speak regularly at sports clubs, charity events and schools. I have spoken to audiences of fewer than ten and audiences of several hundred and I still can't quite believe I have overcome one of my biggest fears. There is always a moment in each talk when I come out of myself and can hear my voice resonating into silence, and I think: *Is that really me?* It is, and if there is one thing I have learned in this whole experience it is that being defeated in life is optional. If you set your mind to something and work hard to achieve it, fears can be overcome and personal success reached. It has given me a confidence I never knew I had.

Working for Saracens opened up my life in ways that I hadn't thought possible. But by the end of 2014, I had a niggling feeling that I hadn't much more to contribute, that I was churning out articles, that my writing was getting stuck, my voice and analysis no longer fresh, and that I should probably concentrate more on my talks. I asked for some time off to think about what I wanted to do and, as usual, Edward and his team were incredibly accommodating, giving me a three-month break and finding someone else to fill in for me.

It was a few weeks later, when I was stuck in bed, waiting impatiently for a sore on my back to heal, that I found what was to open the next chapter of my life.

7

The art of striving gives meaning

LYING IN BED WAITING for a stubborn bedsore to heal is never nice. Every twenty minutes or so I had to lie on one side to air my back, then turn over onto the other side and then sit up with cushions behind me to keep the pressure off. All this changing of position meant my carer had to keep moving me, crossing my legs, uncrossing my legs, turning me round, heaving me up, and it was driving me mad. And I was so bored. Bored out of my mind. Only when I was sitting up could I use my iPad and that also involved a lot of help – getting cushions on my lap, the iPad on the cushions – and anyway, there were only so many games I could play or TV shows I could watch.

One morning, trawling through various apps, I came across a really basic drawing one and downloaded it. I'd always loved art when I was young but started to fall out of love with it as I got older – I did it at GCSE and AS Level – and I was curious to see if I could use the app with my mouth stick. I'd been using a mouth stick for some time – we'd seen it on the Christopher Reeve website – and my Dad, who had become massively adept at adapting things for me, had got a stylus and stuck it on the end which allowed me to type and now draw. In fact, my family had mentioned I might want to give drawing a try when they saw the incredible array of mouth paintings on the walls of Stoke Mandeville Hospital but, in my old characteristic way of not wanting to try in case I failed, I hadn't taken much notice. I had a picture of the Jonny Wilkinson World Cup drop goal on my iPad and so I attempted to copy that. It took ages. The screen was small and my stylus, which was wide at the drawing end, wasn't particularly accurate. As I was in a tetchy mood, at first it all seemed a bit impossible. But as I got into it, clicking between the app and the picture of Jonny Wilkinson until I could recreate it from memory and the drawing took shape, I remembered how much I loved art and how long it was since I'd done any; so I persevered and shared the end result on social media.

People liked it and that really gave me a boost. It's always nice when those you don't know take the trouble to send kind or positive comments, as it makes you feel supported. I'd been tweeting and Facebooking a bit about how I saw things from my perspective, what my life was like and how I'd found ways to adapt and be positive about my situation, and mostly I got really nice replies and comments. But I'd also received some vicious responses, ranging from the implication that I must be lying – how could I be tweeting if I couldn't use my arms? – to the most hateful, a few months after I started drawing, from a woman who told me I 'should have died' and 'didn't deserve' to be able to use my arms and legs after diving into shallow water. I was always shocked that people could behave that way but I decided early on to deal with them in a measured and calm manner, not to provoke them further, but to hopefully make them see that kindness is always the way.

Encouraged by those who liked my drawing and relieved that the concentration required to complete it was distracting me from being laid up in bed, I chose the image of Lewis Hamilton after he won the Formula One World Championship for my second go. I was definitely getting more adept at using the app but in the middle of my next drawing, of Chris Hoy, it shut down. Because I'd had to stop and start so often, I'd got used to saving my pictures but when I downloaded the app again, it turned out you couldn't upload any of your previous drawings.

One of the best things since my accident has been the acquisition of a degree of patience combined with taking time to think around a problem. Instead of abandoning the idea of drawing and moving on, as I might have done in the past, I searched for more apps and found one called Sketch. It had a wide collection of painting tools and a huge range of colours. I continued to draw pictures of the sports men and women whom I'd always admired and soon my bedsore had healed and I was back downstairs, feeling well both physically and mentally. It seemed that drawing was giving me a sense of purpose and I continued, getting bolder in my ambition.

One day, Martin and Charlotte, friends of my parents, came to visit and were looking at my drawings on the iPad. Martin said he might be able to build an easel that I could use from my wheelchair. It was immensely touching how people were still trying to find things that could help me and when he came back a couple of weeks later with a great big wooden construction that I could be pushed into, with the board in front of me and a stand around me, I felt so overwhelmed that I decided there and then to try drawing on paper.

I searched online for mouth sticks to which I could attach pens, pencils and paintbrushes, and found some really cool ones that were light and relatively straightforward to use. I then started drawing with one of those and, once I'd found my feet, I really liked it. The first picture I drew was of Rory McIlroy, to auction at a charity golf day that a friend of ours wanted to organise. He had wanted the day to be a fundraiser for me, but as I felt so fortunate with the money available to me from my trust, I suggested that they did it for the UK Stem Cell Foundation. I'd given a talk to the guests and now I was also able to donate something to the auction. I was worried the drawing wouldn't get any bids, which would have been awkward, and I was massively relieved when it went for a reasonable sum.

This gave me some confidence that what I was producing wasn't too terrible, and after that I was away, drawing every day, sometimes for hours, still focusing on pencil portraits. I'd found that the best way to start was with the eyes, as for me they captured the essence of a person, and then I worked on building from there, not adding too many details to the face but trying to bring out what made the person who they were. It was, funnily enough, my portrait of Audrey Hepburn – my first ever commission – that got a lot of attention on social media; even some requests to buy it.

After a few months I received some commissions and then Leckey, the company that made my wheelchair, saw them online and offered me a specially adapted easel that meant I could start painting. Four months after I started using the iPad for drawing, this opened up yet another world and I soon stopped sketching anything out first and went straight ahead with the paintbrush, which gave me tremendous freedom. I used watercolour paints as they are the most forgiving, and the ability to clean the brush and continue, rarely having to change it, allowed me to focus much better.

Painting at the table in our front room, which has loads of windows through which the light streams in, meant I didn't have to use artificial light and I found that I worked best if I started around midday, generally continuing for four or five hours until a painting was done. My carer would wheel me as close to the easel as I needed to be, place my arms on the cushions on my lap, put a cloth across my arms so that I could dry my brushes, spread a blanket on the floor to prevent it from getting stained with paint, turn on the radio to a music station and leave. I still like being alone as I paint, mostly so I can really zone in on the subject I am painting, and I generally don't stop until I've finished, though I have to be careful not to injure myself. Bending forward to dry the brushes and reach for the paint and water and then straightening up again to the canvas can hurt my neck and the very top of my back, and I have to be careful not to put too much pressure on my core muscles.

Using paint is very different from using pencil and, as I remembered techniques I'd learned about at school, I began to experiment with colour and layers, switching to smaller brushes that enabled me to add more depth and light. Now I was accepting commissions, some of which included animals and landscapes, I had to be flexible and it took me a while to feel comfortable exploring these new subjects.

The staff and pupils at Dulwich were still very much involved, and interested, in my progress and I was asked if I would like to hold a private viewing at the school in the autumn, 14 October 2015. They'd just opened a brand-new three-storey science block with a stunning, light-filled atrium that had as its centrepiece the boat that Sir Ernest Shackleton, an Old Boy of the school, and his men had used to survive a tricky voyage to the Antarctic. It took a bit of self-persuasion that my pictures were anywhere near good enough to show but, since life after my accident was all about opening new doors and making the most of every opportunity, however unlikely, I said yes.

Just before the private view I was commissioned to draw a picture of Chris Robshaw, captain of the England rugby team, for the front cover of 'The Scrum', *The Times*'s World Cup supplement. Even after I'd sent it to the art editor I didn't really think they'd use it, so when I was given a finished copy of the magazine, I had to take a few deep breaths to steady myself. I got some really nice comments about it and requests for a print. Like adding layers of paint, this gave me more confidence leading into my exhibition.

Getting ready for the exhibition was a bit pressurised. We decided on a total of twenty-four paintings, enough to make the space look full. This meant a whole new world of framing and transporting and hanging, and when my pictures were up in this magical new place, I was actually pretty chuffed. The school had invited various guests, and I gave a short talk about my art. As I had my usual out-of-body thing of hearing myself speak, for the first time ever while talking in public my voice cracked and I was overcome with emotion. I don't know what it was about that particular occasion; maybe that the moment had come so quickly and all these people were actually there to see my paintings. I'd recently started making limited prints of my favourites and that evening I sold loads. For days after I thought I'd dreamed the whole thing.

Since the art had begun to take off, along with requests for talking, I found that I needed some help with organisation and admin. Diane was someone we knew previously who had helped in events that had been organised for me and was making my life so much easier. I asked her what she thought about another exhibition and she suggested the Grove, a hotel and conference venue not far from my house. She rang them and, maybe because I lived nearby and they'd seen some local press about my art, they offered us their brand new extension totally free of charge. We decided on a private view on the 8th and my first ever public exhibition on 9 July 2016.

Displaying twenty-four paintings at my old school

had been a big enough challenge. Holding a public exhibition was something I had never planned in my life. But, then again, what of my life was now planned? We worked out that I would need around fifty paintings to fill the space and, for the next few months, I painted almost constantly. And I panicked. I'd paint and I'd panic and sometimes I felt it was all too much. This time the organisation was down to us – who to invite, how to host the private and public viewings, how to sell my prints. What if no one came? What if no one came even if they were invited?

The build-up was not good and several times I wondered if I'd run away with myself, gone beyond what I could realistically achieve. I kept waking during the night with a tight chest and I thought it was anxiety, nerves – not physical at all – and didn't tell anyone. I had no time for being ill or weak and put my tight chest down to all the bending and stretching I had to do in order to paint.

The other thing that was causing me a bit of worry was that the Grove had asked me to invite a few famous faces along. As the space was brand new they wanted to show it as widely as possible and I was really happy to help, so I got in touch with my contacts, mostly rugby players, TV and sports journalists, messaging them and explaining what the evening was about. Much to my astonishment, several said they would come. As the exhibition approached I couldn't quite believe any of them would turn up and I was anxious to ensure my friends and family were on hand to talk to them and make them feel as welcome as possible.

I called my exhibition *Hand to Mouth*, because of the obvious connection of having once been able to use my hands but now having to use my mouth, and because living hand to mouth means living with limited resources, mine being my movement. When we came to hang the paintings, my mum patiently (and impatiently) took instructions from me: *No, turn it a fraction of a millimillimetre to the left* – until we had hung the whole exhibition. The annexe was beautiful, a shining glass extension that allowed light to flood the room.

Despite my worries, several of the 'names' I'd invited turned up, which created quite a buzz. I'd decided to keep the main exhibition space shut while

I gave a short talk in the foyer, where we had hung some of my phrase-paintings, as well as a video of me at work painting some of phrases. Then, once I'd given my speech, we opened the doors to the exhibition space, which gave the whole thing a bit of drama, especially with a big screen of me painting 'Hawkeye' – my painting of a hawk. Once all that was done I began to relax and the evening passed in a whirl of talking. I managed to speak to all of the 150 or so guests and arrived home after midnight, exhausted but exhilarated.

The next day was beautifully sunny and, while ordinarily after a night out I would rest through the following day, I was back at the Grove at midday for the public viewing, anxious all over again that no one who had been invited would come. But I was wrong. Over the course of the day close to a thousand people came – queuing patiently, some waiting ages to talk to me, and so many buying prints that we nearly sold out of some of them. I talked to visitors for six and a half hours without a break, running high on excited disbelief and adrenaline.

I had Diane, Dom, his girlfriend and a friend of his

to take orders. The three paintings that proved the most popular were 'The Gorilla', 'The Lion' and 'Audrey Hepburn'. We sold out of those prints within a couple of hours or so and in hindsight we should have made lots more. I also like to sign my limited prints, so I was looking forward to signing over 250 of them. And because of the space and the stunning grounds at the Grove, people made a bit of a day of it, popping in to the exhibition and then having lunch or a walk around the gardens.

Going home that night I was completely wiped out and, when I'd come down from the high of the exhibition, it became clear that my tight chest I'd kind of been ignoring was not going away. After the exhibition we'd gone down to Dorset and within a few moments of sitting out in the sunshine, something I normally love and can tolerate happily, my skin went bright red and I was overcome by cold, so much so my teeth began to chatter. For the next few hours I was unable to stop shaking and my parents had to call the paramedics. The antibiotics they gave me didn't help and I was so ill I vomited blood. To cut a long story short, for the next week or so I was extremely unwell, the first time I had been seriously unwell since I'd left hospital and I felt worse than I had that day my cousins came to visit and I hadn't been able to see them. Never again was I going to ignore chesty feelings.

My recovery was slow and this marked the beginning of a realisation that I had to pace myself, that the more I was achieving and the greater the demands on my time, the more careful I had to be to retain my core health and mental well-being. Trying to maintain my physio regime as well as meeting deadlines for the exhibition was exhausting and this experience taught me I didn't have to be quite so hard on myself, that collapsing into illness would take me three steps back.

But I couldn't have asked for more from the exhibition – the venue, the numbers who attended, the way my family and friends worked together to make sure my needs and wishes were met, and I was, in moments of quiet reflection, still fairly dazed that I had managed to complete enough paintings and that they had been so well received. But getting all the paintings done, on top of the commissions I had accepted prior to the exhibition, on top of the chest infection and the emotional strain of worrying that no one would come, had almost done me in and I decided to scale things down a bit.

I had been accepting commissions for a while. At the start these had come from family and friends but since I had put my art up on my website, queries had been coming in from members of the public, mostly for pictures of their pets, family or things that meant a lot to them. My favourite commission so far had been from two friends, Josh and Lizzie, a couple who had, independently and unknown to each other, asked me to paint a picture for the other. I'd had to put them on hold until after the exhibition but as soon as I could I returned to the job. Lizzie had commissioned a painting of Josh's dad spraying champagne over him as he completed the London marathon, and Josh had commissioned one of the estuary from the Clifton Suspension Bridge, where they'd had their first date at a bar while at uni in Bristol. There's a balloon festival there every year and so I painted that into the picture, and it turned into a colourful and happy painting that I was really pleased with. It had been the most complicated picture I'd done because of the dead straight bridge, and capturing the perspective from it and getting the angles right had been a challenge.

Because I'd had to delay giving them their paintings and they were both birthday presents, they had had to tell each other what they had done. I invited them both round at the same time and it was so cool when they each saw what the other had commissioned. I had my old easel out, with the painting from Josh to Lizzie, and the one from Lizzie to Josh on my 'new' easel: I first revealed one, then the other. I felt like a proper artist unveiling his work, relieved I'd pleased my clients and been able to keep it all a surprise.

Most of my commissions have been enjoyable to paint. I usually get people to send me a few photos so I can decide which one works best for me. I spend time studying them and getting to know the subject as well as I can. People's pets are especially satisfying to paint. One girl, the sister of a friend of mine from prep school whom I hadn't spoken to for years, emailed to ask me to paint a picture of their dogs for his birthday. One of the dogs had passed away the year before but, as they'd been their childhood pets and the dogs had been incredibly close to each other, I Photoshopped them together and managed to convey them looking close and snuggly – and alive! The toughest commission I accepted after the suspension bridge was of a sailboat, not just because I had to paint it sideways to accommodate the height of it, but also because I got the colour of the sail so wrong and nothing I did could make it right. I had to begin all over again, something I have only ever had to do three times.

There are some things I can't paint and I have had to turn down some requests, such as paintings of a group of people. In order to get everyone in I would have to make their faces quite small and there comes a point when too much detail in a tiny space is too difficult for me to maintain. I did paint a father and his two children, though, because it was so touching. The man was looking down at his children so his face wasn't too detailed, and the children were really young so they were relatively easy to capture.

Some of my commissions make me want to pinch myself. After my accident, the Matt Hampson Foundation had adopted me as one of their beneficiaries and I'd benefitted hugely from this, receiving a cross-trainer from money they'd raised for me. Matt, or Hambo as he is known, was injured during an England under-21s rugby training session in 2005 and was paralysed from the neck down, reliant on a ventilator for his breathing. He set up his foundation to help others injured through sports, and his ethos – Get Busy Living – combined with his generosity, vision and dedication to helping others had had such a positive effect on me that as soon as I could I became an enthusiastic champion of his work, honoured to play whatever role I could. When he told me that Sainsbury's wanted to use my paintings for its 2017 calendar, I was over the moon. They asked me if I would add new paintings of Paralympians and I chose Ellie Simmonds, David Weir and Jonnie Peacock, three sporting legends. The foundation has just begun building the Get Busy Living Centre, a new state-of-the-art rehabilitation facility, and the proceeds from my calendar go directly to that.

More than anything else I do, I feel most defined by my art but, when people ask me if I think of myself as an artist, I can't reply yes without hesitating a moment or two. I feel that you earn the honour of being an artist after you've been doing it for a while and I am still working my way towards that point. On my social media profile I do refer to myself as a mouth artist and that is what I am. But I don't think I've quite earned the title of artist just yet. It's only been a couple of years since I lay in bed experimenting with drawing apps and I am definitely still learning about techniques and different paints, still developing my style.

This much I do know: adversity has given me a gift; enabled me to discover an ability that I would never have otherwise known existed. And for that, I am deeply grateful.

8

Every day is a good day

I WAS SURPRISED THAT the phrase-paintings I'd put up in the foyer of my *Hand to Mouth* exhibition went down so well and caused so much discussion – on the day itself, and afterwards, as people bought the prints. I'd thought carefully about the words but didn't expect them to have such an impact. Reflecting on it now, I suppose they gave people more direct access to my thoughts than through an image or picture, and that the words I chose – 'Accept and Adapt'; 'Be

Grateful'; 'The Little Big Things' and 'Every Day is a Good Day' – were insights into my state of mind and body, as well as my outlook on life.

There seem to be many aspects of my situation and my disability that engage people – from how I manage simple day-to-day tasks to how I'm able to remain so positive – and the words I painted seemed to capture some of these. I came late to the power of words. I wasn't a big fan of English literature at school and only read the occasional book, mostly sport biographies. It was while I'd been lying in the hospital bed reading and rereading all the words that had been so carefully and thoughtfully chosen to express the shock, compassion, hope and love for what had happened to me, that I had the time and capacity to really let the power of words sink in and settle.

Since then I've tried to harness something in the way I express myself when speaking about my situation, especially through my talks. You can say things in any number of words but saying them in the right way – which simultaneously conveys how you are feeling and what you want to communicate, while remaining true to yourself – is difficult and, while I am still striving towards finding all the right words in my talks or on my website, the ones I chose to paint meant a great deal to me.

'Accept and Adapt' were words I'd found easily, as they represent the very foundation of my journey. We all get put in tough situations and have to deal with adversity at some point in our lives, some more profoundly than others, but dealing with difficulty is different from facing it head on and accepting it. You might be struck by an illness or a sudden change in circumstances and find yourself getting through the days by dealing with the practicalities, but if your mind is only focused on hoping things will get better or denying the inevitable outcome, you will soon hit a brick wall. It is, I believe, only when you *accept* that diagnosis – and the prognosis – that you can truly move on.

Up to the point when I first got into the wheelchair at Stoke Mandeville, because I hadn't actually seen myself yet, thoughts had been lurking around in my mind that maybe everything would be OK and when I was 'better', I would get up off the bed, walk out of the door and resume my pre-Portugal life. But when I saw myself in those glass doors and realised the extent and severity of what had happened; after that long day's night of distress when I reached a low I didn't know was down there; I found acceptance. Realising I couldn't go any lower, I decided that I may as well just get on with it and face my situation. I guess, for me, acceptance came once I'd let everything go and I'd reached the bottom, and the only way to regain any sort of life was to turn my back on that darkness and move towards the light. And even to this day, there is no doubt in my mind that when it comes to all the many things I have had to face and do since my accident, accepting my situation was the single most difficult thing I did.

Acceptance gives you the permission and power to move on and, once you move on, you can adapt. Being paralysed from the neck down meant on one level I had no choice but to adapt – how could I not? – but accepting and taking control mentally over how I adapted gave me an internal strength and a much wider range of options and opportunities going forward. I've had to learn a very different way of living and everything I do is about adapting. Some things, such as using my mouth stick to paint or write or communicate on social media, take a lot of practice to begin with but don't then require too much further adapting; but other things, such as getting to know the limitations of my body, require constant tuning and reviewing and accepting. I now know, after some years of stubbornness insisting I could manage everything, that if during the week I'm going to be out, and I also have commissions to finish or a talk to give, I will need to reduce my physio. Or, that if I'm feeling slightly off, I will need to reduce my workload, move my physio and rest until I feel better. These might not seem like big adjustments but it makes things more manageable. And in this I am no different from anyone else. Everyone needs a rest if things get too hectic and it is OK to admit to myself that I need more rest than other people.

Part of the process of adapting has been to get the balance right between pushing myself in a healthy and meaningful way and *needing* to push myself in order to prove – to me, not others – that I *can* push myself. This has been a gradual process. When I first came home, if you'd told me I wouldn't do physio for a week, I'd have had real difficulty dealing with that, as exercising was one means of control I had, in what were then more limited days, and I would have seen not doing it as a negative thing. But as time has passed and I am in control of more elements of my life and am doing a wider variety of things, I can let some of my routine go, knowing that if I don't exercise this week, there is always next week. It's as true that a healthy mind is a healthy body.

Accepting and adapting has led me in many new and fulfilling directions, but being grateful has informed my attitude along the way. My rather instructive painting 'Be Grateful' received a lot of attention, I suppose because people feel that if I'm grateful and I'm in a wheelchair, they should, on the basis of having their mobility, be grateful for that at the very least. But that's not what being grateful is about. It's not about comparing what I don't have to what you do have. That's far too reductive in my opinion. Being grateful is about looking around, opening our eyes to all the little things that we might take for granted. When I was unable to swallow and so thirsty I didn't know how I was going to get from one minute to the next, having those few seconds of sucking the life out of the sponge my mother was allowed to dip in water made me so grateful I was overcome. I realised I had never *tasted* water before. When I'd been lying on my back for weeks in a windowless room and craved sunlight so much I thought I would wither away without it, and was then taken outside, I didn't know how to process the gratitude I felt for something that I had never even *thought* about.

And take something as basic as warmth. The sunshine, the long summer evenings when the air is still holding the day's heat. Most of us love the spring and summer months and feel better when the cold and darkness are left behind. But for me, since I'm no longer able to control the temperature of my body, it's hard to put into words what a difference warmer weather makes to the quality of my life. For the vast majority of the time, I don't know if I'm hot or cold because I can't feel my body temperature, so stabilising it means I have to wear thermals when I go out and when I'm inside, a hood to prevent myself from getting too cold. If it is cold or even just not warm, I often have to stay in my room – where the heating is on full blast, pretty much knocking everyone else out – and have breakfast up there because I know it is going to take me ages to get to the right temperature anywhere else in the house. So, my gratitude for warmer weather, and in particular the summer, is massive and the weekend the clocks go forward and I know the winter is behind me is a time I relish year after year.

Being grateful for the things we might take for granted is something I am glad I have experienced. It means that I can sit outside and really look around me, taking in the beauty of the trees, the sun on the grass; and if that sounds sentimental, it isn't nearly as mushy as the gratitude I feel for all my family, friends and the people I have met since my accident who see me through, whose unconditional love, support and teamwork are the foundation upon which my life and happiness stand.

But being grateful can be tiring and overwhelming, and it shouldn't be something that paralyses you or takes over every time someone is kind or you see the sun or the stars at night. I wouldn't be able to get through the day if I had to explore my gratitude every time someone did something for me. I say enough thank yous in one day to last a lifetime. For me it's about a way of seeing beyond my disability, to rise above the self-pity in which I could wallow, to look for the positive and to be grateful for what I do have. Being bitter about what I no longer have would grind me down, and to be ground down would be grim.

Of course, it's not all a bed of roses being in a wheelchair, and I would be crazy if I said I was grateful about and for *everything*. It can be immensely frustrating to be dependent on people to do almost everything for me. It can drive me insane not to be able to change positions during the night. It can be frustrating when I have to go through the extent of my needs with a new carer. It can be frustrating when I fall ill with a chest or bladder infection and can't get better as quickly as I used to. And just being in my wheelchair can take a lot out of me.

I am not really supposed to be in a wheelchair without head or arm rests. My wheelchair is not designed for someone with the severity of my paralysis and so sitting in my wheelchair all day is not as easy as it looks. To balance and sit upright, I have to call on the power of the very few working muscles that I have left and it can be ferociously tiring keeping them going. Sitting in it, painting in it, even watching TV, I am never fully relaxed and the effort that takes, combined with my body working overtime to keep me going, contributes to my general fatigue. There are some days when lying in bed seems like a tempting option. But that's not for me and being in my wheelchair is crucial to my ability to determine the way I live and is a great motivator when it comes to exercise. The stronger I am, the more able I am to balance and sit in my chair and I enjoy the freedom it brings me. A wheelchair with a head rest and arm rests can weigh a ton whereas my chair is extremely light and that makes a real difference to my ability to get out and about, making the life of whoever is navigating me up and down stairs, or through crowds, a whole lot easier.

At home, I rest my arms on cushions that are placed on my lap, but when I'm out I tape up my shoulders to keep my joints in place. One of the consequences of being put in the wrong wheelchair, without armrests, was that it caused a subluxation of my shoulder. As I had no muscles to hold the joint in place, the tendons and ligaments stretched, creating a gap in my shoulder joint. It still causes a lot of pain and when someone is moving my arms they have to be very careful. Through targeted exercise, I now have more muscle but because there are still gaps, taping my shoulders helps keep the joints in place which means I can balance in my chair quite comfortably and exercise more vigorously. Taping takes a while and over the course of time I have learned to think ahead, to plan, to have enough time for the taping to be applied, frustrating as that can be.

But frustration isn't the opposite of gratitude and there is often a way around things that frustrate me. It's all a matter of looking at what I can do, not at what I can't. And most importantly, for me at least, being grateful for all the many things I can do makes it easier to show those around me that I am profoundly thankful for all they do for me.

Some of those are 'The Little Big Things' that informed my third painting, because my life has been – and is still being – enriched by people's thoughtfulness and kindness. There isn't a millimetre of doubt in my mind that the unconditional love of my mum, dad and brothers, that endless, bottomless emotional support that they gave me – and each other – during those initial dark days, was what got me through. When I think back and remember – how my dad, whose business was struggling during those recession-gloomy days, came to see me every single night no matter what the stresses of work entailed; how Tom came up from university every weekend no matter what interruption this caused to his studying or social life; how Will, who was setting out on his professional rugby career, would come day in day out, whatever the demands of his training and how Dom, who was studying for his GCSEs, would come after school and do his schoolwork in my room or downstairs in the hospital cafeteria; and how my mum was by my side throughout, my constant companion navigating this bewildering new world for me, for us all – I can barely take it all in. There were no grand gestures, no histrionics, there was no need for anyone to be told: this is what you do, this is what is expected of you, be here, come there, do this, do that. Instead the tide of their love and all the little big things that flowed from that love, rolled out and has kept on rolling ever since. And nowadays, as my disability is our norm, the myriad of little big things that they and others do for me is something I never take for granted. That my *yiayia* and aunt *still* cook my favourite dishes for me, that brothers and my mates are always up for a night out or coming over to watch the rugby or spend time with me, that my parents' friends are still mindful of them, never fails to touch me.

My family and I will never forget those gestures that friends and extended family made while I was in hospital, like leaving food on the doorstep so my brothers would have a proper supper each evening, or sending me cards and messages that still mean so much to us all. I can't really emphasise enough how knowing that people were bearing us in mind, knowing that they were coming up with ways of supporting us through their thoughts or cooking or offers of help, made those dark days a whole light lighter. If I ever hear that a mate or a family member or someone whose story touches me is in distress, I now think of ways in which I can help or send thoughtful words of comfort.

I'm fortunate to have a profile on social media and, while I am happy when people message me with nice comments on my paintings or thoughts I have put out there, the most humbling times are when people reach out to tell me that I have helped them in difficult times, that through reading my story and the ways in which I have accepted and adapted, pushed myself and remained optimistic, they have themselves seen a different way forward. I guess it's a confirmation that the little things I am doing are the right things and, for some people, maybe even the big things.

Because people seem to take notice of some of the things I say, I have recently been encouraged to share my thoughts on wider issues. It feels wrong to me that decisions about disability payments and disability opportunities are made, by and large, by those who don't understand what it's like to be disabled. To me it's straightforward – give someone the care they need and then they can contribute to society; give them the bare minimum and they have to fight to survive and can't contribute. It feels to me and many others that disabled people are being punished for *being* disabled, which feels like total injustice to me. For now, I am more comfortable expressing my beliefs on social media rather than on a wider political platform. But now that I never say never, combined with my belief that, if people do want to listen and I can speak out for others in a similar or less fortunate position than myself, I may well give voice more publicly to my views on the need for improved rights for those living with disability or impairment. Not to do so would be irresponsible.

While I tend to stick to my script when I give my talks, I like to answer questions the audience may have. There are several I am asked on a regular basis, including whether I think I will, through advances in medicine, be able to move my arms or walk again; whether I am able to enjoy a regular social life, go out to clubs, have girlfriends; and what I think lies ahead for me.

When I was first in hospital, in Portugal, my parents were keen to tell me that medical science was an amazing thing; that advances were being made so quickly and incredible things were possible. This, of course, was largely due to the shock they were in, a form of denial of the situation I was in, and the truth was that none of us knew anything about even the basics of spinal cord injuries, let alone any potential advances in treatment. But five years after my accident, medical science and in particular the work of Geoffrey Raisman, a neuroscientist at University College London, who sadly passed away in January 2017, have led to a disabled man being able to walk again. Darek Fidyka, who was left paralysed from the waist down after being knifed outside his home by his wife's ex-husband, is able to walk again with the help of leg braces and a walking frame. In a pioneering operation, Raisman and his team removed some of Mr Fidyka's cells from the nerves that run from his nose to his brain and injected them into the eight-millimetre gap that the knife wound had left in his spine. This has enabled the damaged nerve cells to regrow, restoring his spinal cord, and he now has feeling below his injury in his legs, bowels and bladder. If he continues to make progress he will be the first person to have a spinal cord paralysis reversed by an operation.

All of this was made possible by the transplantation of his own stem cells and, having read up on it,

I am a great believer that stem cells offer the greatest way forward in treating some of the most debilitating conditions out there. I've since become involved with the UK Stem Cell Foundation, fundraising and helping to raise awareness of what they do. There is still a long, long way to go. Mr Fidyka's injury was not as severe as mine – he had the use of his arms – and it is not yet possible to assess the long-term effects of his operation or to see if it works for others. But in answer to the question, 'Do you think you will ever move your arms or walk again unaided?': while the chances are not that high during my lifetime, with the exciting advances being made in stem cell research, for which I am continually grateful, who knows what could happen?

In terms of a social life, I have a great time with my brothers and my mates and enjoy a big night out or going out at the weekend. When I drink I try to remain aware of what is going on around me, especially if everyone else is drinking. But I am always struck by how kind people are to me, gathering around to hoick my wheelchair up or down stairs, making sure I am not feeling left out, helping me in and out of cabs. I find that adults are much more squeamish or reserved about asking what must really be on their minds, whereas schoolchildren are far more able to express their own fears through questions. I have been asked all sorts of things, ranging from how I am able to go to the loo, to how I get food from the plate to my mouth and how I get my trousers on.

But the one thing I am asked most often is this: 'Given your situation, you must have down days – there must be days when you ask yourself, why me?'

And in answering this one I look at whoever asks me the question and I tell them that I wake up every day grateful for everything I have in my life. I look around and think about my incredible family and friends. The life that my parents have given my brothers and me. I get to wake up every day and do a job I love. I get to be challenged to push myself in many ways on many levels and I am always learning, always moving forwards. Not many people can say that and when I look at my life this way, I consider myself very lucky. What do I have to be down about? I have so much to be happy for.

There is no point dwelling on what might or could

have been. The past has happened and cannot be changed; it can only be accepted. Life is much simpler and much happier when you always look at what you can do, not what you can't do.

Every day is a good day.

ACKNOWLEDGEMENTS

Thanks to all those who have contributed to the little big things, that have made life for my family and for me so much happier. There are too many of you to mention by name but you know who you are. We will be forever ever grateful for what you do and what you have done.

Thanks to Neil Blair whose idea this book was. And to my agents Josephine Hayes and Zoe King. Amanda Harris, Olivia Morris and everyone at Orion who made the book possible. Special thanks to Gillian Stern who helped me get my words onto the page and enabled me to tell my story.

ABOUT THE AUTHOR

Henry Fraser is a British artist and motivational speaker. Henry was 17 years old when a tragic accident severely crushed his spinal cord. Paralysed from the shoulders down, he has conquered unimaginable difficulty to embrace life and a new way of living.

Using a specially developed stylus and easel Henry has become an accomplished mouth-painter. His first solo exhibition, Hand-to-Mouth, took place in July 2016. He has produced images for *The Times*' coverage of the 2015 Rugby World Cup and has earned a strong A-list fan base from J.K. Rowling to the England Rugby and England Cricket teams.

★

Henry's 'Pushing Myself' talk inspires a number of high profile businesses and sports teams, including the Saracens and the England 7s. His talk encourages others to step outside of their comfort zones and to find the gifts in life's challenges. Henry perfectly embodies his personal mantra of taking a 'relentlessly positive approach to life' and passionately motivates others to do the same.

He was named on the Power 100 list as the 7th most influential person living with a disability in Britain in 2017.

www.henryfraser.org
www.henryfraserart.com

CHARITIES HENRY SUPPORTS

UK Stem Cell Foundation

www.ukscf.org

Since the dawn of the human species groups of individuals have had their lives lessened or shortened by medical conditions for which there is no solution. Everyday, and despite major medical advances occurring over the last two hundred years, far too many people hear the news that there is no effective treatment for their condition.

In 2006 the UK Stem Cell Foundation was born. Its mission was to advance exciting new cell therapy based treatments toward the clinic and within the reach of individuals with few clinical choices. With the help of financial gifts it has enabled some £25 million of high quality therapy development to occur across the UK.

The Foundation is the only charity dedicated to exclusively advancing stem cell based therapies and only funds research that has potential to be in the clinic within the short to medium term. Using this approach has led to new therapies being placed into a range of clinical trials.

This work is benefiting patients and helping to secure the UK's position in a valuable new industry sector.

MATT HAMPSON FOUNDATION

Matt Hampson Foundation

www.matthampsonfoundation.org

Matt Hampson chose to get busy living after sustaining his life changing injury in 2005.

This is the philosophy behind everything the Matt Hampson Foundation aims to do; we help people get busy living again after a life altering injury. Whether by helping them get back into sport or just assisting in making adjustments to their new life we are there to help and support them on their chosen path. All our beneficiaries are getting busy living and we are very proud of this fact.

OUR PURPOSE To inspire and support young people seriously injured through sport.

OUR MISSION – GET BUSY LIVING To create a support network of people seriously injured through sport and their families to help each other by sharing knowledge and experiences.